SLAYING THE
LAW SCHOOL
DRAGON

SLAYING THE LAW SCHOOL DRAGON

George J. Roth

DODD, MEAD & COMPANY, NEW YORK

1 2 3 4 5 6 7 8 9 10

Library of Congress Cataloging in Publication Data

Roth, George J
    Slaying the law school dragon.

    Bibliography: p.
    1. Law students—United States—Handbooks, manuals,
etc. 2. Law schools—United States. 3. Law—Study
and teaching—United States. I. Title.
KF283.R68   340'.073   80-16974
ISBN 0-396-07880-X
ISBN 0-396-07879-6 (pbk.)

To BETTY AND JEFF

CONTENTS

1
WHY YOU SHOULD READ THIS BOOK

Annually, thousands of new students enter law schools all over the country. A tremendous number never finish. Some drop out; some flunk out. Why?

Essentially, they're all good students and probably have higher than average intelligence. Most are unusually dedicated, determined, and extremely motivated. Some have already had successful careers. Why the high disaster rate? What's the trouble? Can we do anything about it?

Let's answer the last question first, with a great big YES! That's what this book is all about. If you follow my advice, and adapt my suggestions to your own particular personality, the chances are good that you'll be among those who stay in school, pass the bar, and go on to a rewarding professional life. If you would have been a good student without the help of this book, it will make you an excellent one; if you would have been a fair student, it will make you a good one; and if you would have been a poor student, it will give you that extra shove you will need to get you through.

Let's look at a few reasons for the high drop-out statistics.

Obviously, among the thousands who start, there are some people who just aren't temperamentally suited to be law students. It takes a certain ability to think flexibly within a rigidly structured framework; an ability to logically analyze what frequently appears to be an illogical or perhaps inequitable situation; an ability to be extremely serious in approach to what is presented, coupled with the desire, courage, and inclination to readily and periodically laugh at the whole thing, particularly with reference to the individual's own place as a student in the system.

Most law students get so involved in running the law school rat race that they never have time to relax and eat the cheese which is readily available if they could only see it. The basic trouble is that their poor study habits lead only to frustrated exhaustion.

A large part of the problem is caused by the professors. Most of them are not good teachers. In most cases, they are people who have been top students themselves and who have gone into teaching law right out of law school. That's all they know. It's almost genetic—they put out the course material the same way they learned it. They believe that there has always been a large group of students who have failed to finish and, unto all eternity, there always will be. These professors are only interested in the theory of the law; the teaching of it is merely an incidental way of earning a living while affording them the time to delve deeply into the exotic mystiques of their specialty muses.

Oh sure, there usually are some professors on every campus who really love to teach; who thrive on development of the intellectual maturity of their students; who year after year can make the abstract turn into the concrete. But these beloved magicians are rare. They're grossly counterbalanced by the intellectual snobs and academaciated clones who make up the bulk of the American law school faculty army.

This book will show you a way to deal with these tithing teachers—those who give only one-tenth of themselves to their students and keep nine-tenths of themselves for themselves.

2
DON'T LET THEM INTIMIDATE YOU

Intimidation is the law school dragon. It is nurtured on a mother's milk so soured by the catalytic action of incompetent and sadistic professors that its chemical composition is changed from what could be enlightenment and pleasurable acceptance of knowledge into anxiety, inordinate competition, and deep frustration.

The anxiety comes from not knowing what you're doing, not knowing where you stand academically in the class for weeks at a time, and not knowing where you're going to find time to do all the things which are expected of you.

The inordinate competition is engendered by a system of daily recitation which is designed to make you look stupid, cause traumatic embarrassment, and make you feel like you were never cut out to be a lawyer in the first place. The big pitch is to get high grades so you can get a job in a good law firm when you graduate. Every classmate is a potential enemy.

The frustration comes when you can't seem to understand a point of law which is so simple for everyone else, when you don't have time to do the work, and when you don't get the good grades you hoped for.

My first three weeks of law school were utter hell. I didn't know whether I was doing the right thing or the wrong thing. Neither did anybody else.

I got there on the first day of school and found myself already behind. I didn't know that the assignment schedule had been posted in advance. The professor started right out discussing the cases I hadn't read.

Someone said that you had to buy a green hardcover notebook for each subject, one that had a red line down the left side. The idea was to "brief" the cases on the right side and take class notes on the left. I didn't even know what "briefing" meant.

I guess they figured we were graduate students and it was up to us to find out on our own what was expected. Oh, yes, the dean did come in at the start of the first lecture and give a five-minute welcome speech. I'll never forget his great ending: "Look to the right of you; look to the left of you. Next year one of you won't be here. Ha! Ha! Ha!" Later, I found out that it was a national ritual recited on every campus—one of the secret passwords of the fraternity.

Today, many law schools give some type of "orientation." But usually it is so skeletal that it's not much help. One of the things which they could do that would be extremely valuable would be to present a series of lectures giving a quick overview of each of the freshman courses and, if possible, of a number of the other courses offered in subsequent years. These lectures should be given before school actually starts so that the students can have some idea of what's to come and how the different areas of the law fit together.

Since most law schools don't do this, you should do it for yourself. Over the summer, before school starts, go to your local law library and *quickly* skim through some elementary textbooks on Contracts, Torts, Crimes, and Property. Don't try to learn anything—just get some overall feeling of what you're going up against.

I'm going to show you how to study so you can understand what you read and what your professors are talking about; explain how to organize and remember your work; give you tips on how to handle exams; give you the will to combat the professorial put-downs; and help you get the confidence in yourself that will enable you to succeed in law school and, eventually, in practice.

There is an ancient incantation which you will find helpful on your journey. Keep it in front of your eyes. Inscribe it on your walls and doorposts. It will give you strength to meet the challenges which may beset you on your path. It will aid you in combating the law school intimidation syndrome. It will enable you to slay the law school dragon!

ILLEGITIMUS NON CARBORUNDUM

Illegitimus means the parents forgot to get married; *non* means no; and *carborundum* is a grinding stone. Put it all together and it comes out: Don't let the bastards grind you down!

So, put on your best armor; pick your best steed; polish up your best lance—and LET'S GO!

3
WHAT TO DO BEFORE SCHOOL STARTS

Get started four weeks early! There's a lot to do.

Get yourself the best living accommodations you can afford, and get them as close to the law library as possible. That's where you'll be spending most of your after-class hours for the next three years; and the less time you waste trudging back and forth, the more you'll have available for work and study.

Try for a place that's relatively quiet. You'll need as much sleep as you can get, and when you're studying in your room, you'll need an atmosphere that's efficient enough for critical contemplation.

I had a place at the start of my second year of law school that looked pretty good wten I moved in, but after some other students got there, it became a hedonist's dream.

A music major moved in next door. He must have had at least fifty different instruments—Chinese oboe, African drums, Eskimo nose pipes, Argentine kazoos, the whole works. Plus two stereo sets!

The music wasn't too bad at first, when he kept things fairly low. But then romance took over. He started inviting young ladies up to examine his instruments, and after each would arrive, he would introduce her to the esthetic values to be gained by vibrating the bed springs to the rhythms of Brahms, Beethoven, Bach, boogie-woogie, and bossa nova. These music lessons soon expanded into a physics course. He had some of his student contemporaries bang gongs and cymbals at the exact mathematical apex and nadir of the sine curve of the bed spring vibrations.

He was a very hospitable guy, and I found myself over at his place more than mine. Blackstone went down the tubes for a while. If I hadn't moved to new quarters, I'm certain I would have flunked out of school that semester.

Besides your apartment, check out all the cheap restaurants, pizza places, beer joints, water holes, disco dens, and singles bars in the neighborhood. Find out where one or two really good places to dine out are in case you want to impress someone during the semester. Do it now, for you won't have time later.

And don't forget the supermarkets, drug stores, movie theaters, gym facilities, emergency medical set-up, and anything else you think you might need. You can do most of this looking around at night and on weekends during this early preschool period.

On Monday of the first of these four weeks before school officially opens, drop in at the law school. If any professors are there, introduce yourself, have a talk with them, size them up. Say hello to the administrators and the clerical workers in the law school office. Ask everybody you come in contact with if they can give you any tips to help you get through your first year. You never know; occasionally you'll pick up something valuable. Serendipity works in strange and unusual ways.

Get a list of the casebooks which you will be using and then go out and buy them. Make sure you get the right edition. Compare prices off campus with the student book store. In the old days, that was sometimes cheaper. Today, the book store is one of the campus's big money raisers.

Be sure to go into the lecture halls where your classes will be held. Actually sit in several different seats in each one so you know where you'll want to sit when school starts. This environmental impact survey is extremely worthwhile. Some schools now assign seats by computer. Try and change to one you like if you can.

On Tuesday, spend a few hours in the school law library. Talk to any librarians who are around. Most of them are pretty helpful and can give you a great amount of information. Browse around the different parts of the stacks and thumb through the various types of law books. Find out where the best carrels are for you to work. Look for drafty air conditioning outlets; areas where there will be too much extraneous visual stimulation, noise, student traffic, etc. Think of yourself as an early-stage embryo and the library as your womb-home for the next three years. That's really where lawyers come from, you know.

Use Wednesday to visit the local county courthouse. In the morning, ask the clerk to show you how the litigation indices work. Take a look at a few civil and criminal case files.

One thing which may come as a surprise is that a lawsuit ultimately boils down to a bunch of papers. And that bunch of papers is all an appellate court looks at to come to the decision which you read in your casebook.

Don't, however, try to get very much out of what's in all these papers. Just notice the titles: Complaint, Temporary Restraining Order, Demurrer, Answer, Motion, Order, etc.; see that there's always some controversy which people are fighting about. Note that everything is presented in some formal way. All of this will give you a better comprehension of what you'll be studying about later on; you'll find it to be interesting as well as informative. While you're at it, you'll also see that some lawyers seem to have put more work into their cases than others. While it's not always true, it usually works out that the ones who win are the ones who are most thoroughly prepared.

Leave all of that afternoon for a visit to the county law library. It's usually in the courthouse. Some libraries have a full-time law librarian; in others, the librarian is the judge's secretary.

Try to become as friendly with the librarian as possible, for this person can be of invaluable help to you throughout your entire law school career. When a professor assigns some outside reading, for example, and two hundred of your classmates line up waiting for the only copy in the university law library, this friend can rapidly get a copy for your use, either from his or her own library, or through the state library book exchange.

This librarian can save you the outdated advance sheets—the paperback copies of printed decisions which come out before the final bound volumes. And you can use these to build up your own home library, which will only be a year behind the bound volumes all the way through law school.

Never take any book away from the county law library without the *express,* clearly understood permission of the county law librarian. Not only would it sour your relations when the librarian gets chewed out by the judge because some needed book is unavailable, but it's also a felony in many states; and some overzealous young deputy D.A. might just think it would be fun to prosecute you.

If some more enterprising persons have already asked this librarian to pledge the advance sheets to them ahead of you, you might try stopping in at the big law firms around town to see if they will give you this material. It's just another source to tap and could possibly help you make a contact which might result in a job in later years.

If there's a state appellate court anywhere nearby, visit it. Chances are, it won't be in session—usually they meet only once a month to hear oral argument, and frequently there is no calendar during the summer months. When you do go, be sure to look at some of the files. Generally, you will find that each file contains a copy of the trial court clerk's record, a stenographic transcript of the trial testimony, and the appellate briefs filed by each side. Completed cases will also contain a copy of the court's opinion. It is an opinion like this which gets into the law school casebooks and it is the kind of material you'll be using every day of your law student career.

4

BROWSING AROUND THE LAW BOOKS

Before we go any further and I tell you how to use up the rest of the four-week period before school starts, it will be necessary for you to know something about the different kinds of law books which you will be using.

Words are about the only tools a lawyer has. So, until you become an expert at using them, you'll remain a poor craftsman; what you must try to become is an artist. Put another way, unless you quickly get comfortable with legal jargon, things will be mighty rough.

The first thing you'll have to have is a good legal dictionary. This is a must. There are several standard works available. Personally, I like Black's, published by West Publishing Company. And if you can get one secondhand, even if it's an older edition, by all means do so. The definitions you'll work with are mostly a couple of hundred years old, so it won't matter if the one you have is nice and modern, or old and dusty. But get one with a fairly good binding. You'll use it all through law practice, too.

The legal dictionary is different from the regular dictionary. Besides English words, it has all the Latin phrases used in the law and defines the legal meaning of each—not according to Noah Webster or Samuel Johnson, but cited (referenced) to some case, whenever possible, where a court in an appellate decision has said that's what the particular word or expression means.

At this point, let me emphasize something: You don't need to be a Latinist to study law. Anything you'll need to use in a foreign language can be looked up in a law dictionary. And, today, courts rarely use Latin expressions. If you're ever in court and the judge uses one you've never come across before, politely ask for an explanation of the reference. The judge will probably apologize and tell you what it means with no hard feelings.

Which brings me to how cases get into the law books. Schematically, a case usually starts out somewhere "down below" when two people get into an argument that they can't settle. Eventually, one sues the other and the case comes to court. The jury or the judge gives a verdict for one of them. The losing party is dissatisfied and appeals.

Each side files briefs with the appellate court (no jury here)—usually a panel of three judges in intermediate appellate courts, with five or seven sitting on most state supreme courts, if the case gets that high. The cases are argued orally before the appellate court (no witnesses either), which then gives a written decision.

This decision is called a ruling or a holding. While its effect is that one side generally wins the case, in reality it is only a holding as to whether the lower court correctly decided the case.

Whatever the result, the case is transferred (remanded) back to the lower court—the trial court—for final disposition in accordance with the appellate court's ruling.

If the case comes up through the federal court system, it is first tried in a district court, appealed to a circuit court, and ultimately to the United States Supreme Court.

It is this written decision, the opinion of an appellate court, which is set forth in your law school casebooks. Frequently, however, it is shortened by the casebook editor who only leaves what he or she considers pertinent to establish some point he or she wishes to make.

In actuality, the opinion of the court, commonly referred to as the "case," is printed in full in a book which is one volume of that particular state's (or the federal) reports.

Sometimes a state will have more than one set of reports. In California, for example, because of the huge number of cases, the intermediate appellate court decisions are published as the California Appellate Reports, while the state supreme court cases appear in the California Reports. These reports are often called the official reports because they are published under the authority of the particular court system that issues the decisions.

One tricky thing to be aware of is that the highest appellate court in most cases is known as the supreme court, but in New York it is called the court of appeals. In that state, the local trial courts are called superior courts.

Each case in the reports is designated by funny cryptographiclike numbers and letters called "citations." Let's suppose that Charles Hogan sued William Zirp in a California court, and that it was appealed to the intermediate appellate court, called the court of appeals. If it did not go any further, the court's opinion would appear in some volume of the California Appellate Reports. For this hypothetical example, let's say it was in 1886. At that time, perhaps, the publisher had only reached volume fifteen. If this case were printed starting at page 197, then the citation (where to find it) would read *Hogan* v. *Zirp* (1886) 15 Cal. App. 197. The citation gives us the name of the case, the year the decision was rendered, the volume and name of the appellate case reports in which it is printed, and the page on which it starts. Sometimes the names on appeal are reversed from what they were in the trial court. It depends on what state you're in as to which style is used. At first, this party-name reversal may be a little confusing, but as long as you're aware of the practice, you shouldn't have any problem.

In the old English reports, usually the name of the set of reports is taken from the name of the reporter, the person who edited the series. Sometimes it's taken from the name of the court. Many of these old English cases show the plaintiff as *Rex* v. ———, or *Regina* v. ———. This does not mean that Rex or Regina were unusually litigious persons. Rex means King; Regina means Queen. In the United States the term *State* v. ———, or *People* v. ———, is customarily used when the state government is bringing the law suit; *United States* v. ——— when the federal government is involved.

Which brings me to the next book you should get. Like the legal dictionary, you'll use this throughout law school, and in your law office practice as well. I'm talking about a book on how to do legal research, how to find out what the law is in some very particular area. There are several good books in the field. Most give a good discussion of the various reports and statutes, have sample pages so you can actually see what they are referring to, and tell you in detail how to look up the law. Before you buy any of these, make sure that, if your law school gives a legal research course, you buy the one that will be used there. But scan some of the others in the library, anyway. You may find they're clearer to follow. One of the best ones I've seen is Price and Bittner, *Effective Legal Research,* published by Prentice-Hall.

Now, what other kinds of law books are there?

First, there are the reports I talked about before. These come out chronologically. You'll be using cases from England, and the different states of this country. The West Publishing Company puts out a series of regional reports containing the cases for geographically grouped states so that lawyers in one can see what is happening in adjacent areas (Northeastern, Southwestern, Southern, Pacific, etc.).

A recent development in law is the use of computers for research. The cases in various sets of reports are put into memory banks verbatim. Then, through word analysis, citation, or some other code, are made retrievable as required.

There are also index books to find the cases in which you are interested. The reporter who compiles the reports usually summarizes each major point involved in a case in a short sentence or paragraph printed at the beginning of the case. This is called a headnote. Each one is given a number. The numbers are inserted into the running text of the decision so you can easily find the particular language that interests you.

The headnotes are arranged by subject matter in books called digests. The subject matter is usually factually oriented, and if the digest index is good, a case in point on the subject matter in which you are interested, if one exists, can readily be found.

When you look up a case in a digest you will always find the headnote has a citation to a report. Having that, you can then go back, find the case in the report, and read it at length.

At the back of the digest, there is a table of all cases referred to in the compiled headnotes. If you know the name of a case and need the citation, you can obtain it from the table of cases. Also, this table will direct you to each place in the digest where the particular headnotes from every case are located. This means that, if you have the name of a case, you can first find where it is referred to in the digest; then, by turning to that section, you will find all the other cases in that state on the same point.

Don't forget, however, that the digest only contains the cases for the period of time and the particular state or area that it covers. In other words, if you're in the New York Digest, you won't find any Ohio case listed or described.

If you have a citation for an American case, there are a series of valuable books known as *Shepards' Citations* which you can use for finding cases in point. These books contain tables of numbers. You get the volume of *Shepards'* for the state or area you're interested in, look up the volume number of the report in which your case appears, then run down the column until you reach the proper page reference—and that's it. At that place, you'll find a citation to every place where the case is mentioned. There are also different symbols printed next to each of these reference citations which show whether each point in the original case was overruled, agreed with, distinguished, modified, etc.

Next for consideration are textbooks. These give an analysis of the law in one subject like Contracts, Torts, Corporations, Criminal Procedure, etc. Some are in one volume, others are sets. Generally, each sentence or phrase in a textbook is a summary of the particular holding in some case which is printed in full somewhere in the different reports. The footnotes in the textbook give the citations where the case referred to may be found. A valuable one-volume series of textbooks for students are called "hornbooks." These have lead paragraphs or sentences in boldface type emphasizing some principle of law, followed by, in lighter type, a discussion citing the relevant cases in point.

Encyclopedias are many-volumed sets containing a discussion of practically every phase of every law subject. The two great national works are *American Jurisprudence 2nd* and *Corpus Juris Secundum.* Similarly, the publishers put out other encyclopedias giving only the law of a particular state.

In the old days, all law books were tan, leather-covered works. Today, they come in many colors. There's a great story about the lawyer who worked for a firm for fifty years. He was one of the best in the office. Each day, he would come to work, unlock his desk, look at a little piece of paper inside, mutter to himself, and then carefully lock the drawer again before commencing his work. One day he suddenly died. All the other lawyers rushed over to his desk, broke the lock, and studied the paper to see if they could find the secret of success the old man had kept hidden these many years. It read: "West's is blue, Deering's is red."

Along with the general group of textbooks is a group called Restatements of the Law. These are written by a national assembly of professors who watch current changes in broad, legal principles and then write a suggested interpretation which they hope will be adopted across the country. One of the best things about the Restatements for law students is that they contain a number of factual situations written in simple language to illustrate the point they wish to make. A word of caution, however: Don't try to read the technical explanations too early in your law school career as you probably won't understand what they are talking about. Just read the boldface type and the short examples.

The law as a whole is divided, generally, into two parts: constitutions, statutes, ordinances, regulations, on the one hand; and what the judges say these mean, their interpretations, on the other. The reports in the casebooks that I have been talking about are the judges' interpretations. Judge-made law is also sometimes referred to as "modern common law."

There are a whole group of books which give us the laws enacted by Congress, state legislatures, county boards of supervisors, city councils, district commissions, etc., along with the administrative regulations of operating departments of each of these branches of government. They usually are called "codes." There are two types, annotated and unannotated. Annotated codes have citations to cases where they are discussed; unannotated codes are basically printed just as they are enacted.

Practically every law school in the country puts out something called a law review. It usually contains a few long articles by experienced lawyers and professors about various legal subjects and also has notes written by students about recent developments in the law. Law reviews are good to use to get ideas on new trends and concepts. Frequently, something suggested in a law review article is adopted later as the basis of a decision by some court. These articles customarily are full of citations to numerous cases in the area of law they are discussing. In the Selected Law Review Articles at the end of this book, I've made a compilation of over a hundred law reviews which will be extremely valuable to you. Browse through the titles when you get a chance. They won't mean anything to you now, but at least you'll know what kind of excellent research material exists when you need it later.

One additional thing. Around every law school campus, commercially produced subject outlines continuously surface. Most of these come from bar review courses, sometimes called "quiz" courses. Try to get the ones most students use at the school you go to. They can be invaluable for exam review as well as daily study. Ignore any professor's admonition not to use them. Just don't let your professors know that you do.

5
HOW TO GET READY FOR CLASS

If you followed the suggestions in the third chapter, you should still have a little better than three and a half weeks left before school starts. Used properly, this period can be the most productive of the entire semester. This is the time which should be spent in getting ready for your classes.

What you do now will set the stage for the whole year. It will put you ahead of your fellow students and will give you the time to handle other extra curricular work which is essential to your successful progress in law school.

For each course you take, you will find that at least one good textbook exists. The librarian can provide you with these. Most of the cases in your casebook for that course will be cited in the textbook, particularly if the same person authored both. If you compare the table of contents of the text and casebooks and then browse through both, you will notice that each sentence in the text is cited to a case which is likely to be in your casebook.

The law school casebook is really a developmental exposition of a particular subject; instead of telling you what the law is, however, you have to read the cases and figure it out for yourself. In the textbook, the author tells you what the law is and cites the cases in footnotes for his authority.

The first step is to find the rule of each case (what it "holds," what it means) in the textbook and write it in the margin of the casebook, across the top of the page. Don't bother to read the case at this point, just put down the rule.

If you can't find the case in the textbook, you may have to look it up in the reports; you can do this with the citation that appears under the name of the case. Use the headnote that seems to apply to the subject of the course. Go through the casebook and mechanically do this rule writing as fast as you can. You'll probably need two or three days for each course. Plan your time so you get a bit ahead in each casebook, even if you can't finish all of them. Later, you'll probably be able to squeeze in some extra time to complete the job. If you can get all the casebooks done earlier, however, you'll have it a lot easier when minutes are precious.

If you haven't realized it by now, before you begin classes, you'll already have read a textbook of the full course once and, even though you have done so very superficially, you also have written down all the major information which that textbook has to offer.

Your professors will say you can't learn what the case holds unless you go through the discipline of digging it out for yourself. I disagree. I think you can. Not only more quickly, but in a fashion that makes it easy to remember and simple to comprehend.

Let me tell you a little story from my post-law-school past. Some years ago, my eldest son became a Boy Scout and I inherited the scoutmaster's job. One of my duties was to teach the kids how to tie six different knots. If you think that's an easy task, try it. After three weeks, most of these eleven-year-old kids couldn't complete the work. Then I tried an experiment. I remembered how I studied in law school when I wrote the rule down before I read the case.

I got some heavy three-quarter-inch rope and tied all the knots. The kids were instructed to *open* the knots slowly, then retie them. Within fifteen minutes, every one of the tenderfeet could expertly tie every one of the six knots. Later on, when they had to learn harder knots, they had no trouble figuring out how, just from reading the instruction book. They learned the *theory* of knot tying. After that, I always taught new kids to tie knots in a few minutes instead of a few weeks.

So, as you'll see a little later on, you'll read the case to see how they got to the rule, not to figure out what the rule is. After you've had lots of experience, you'll have no trouble reading a case and picking out the rule without looking in a text or using the headnotes. In fact, later on you should only use the headnotes to help you focus in on the specific part of a case in which you are interested. But as a study device, it's very helpful to use them as I have suggested.

The next thing to do is to study the table of contents for each course. Look up all unfamiliar terms in your law dictionary. Write the definitions in the margin. Don't put any time into trying to memorize these definitions. At this stage, you're only trying to get a broad overview of the entire course so you'll be able to see right from the beginning where everything will fit in. You should, however, memorize the major headings in the table of contents. More about this later.

Under the customary law school method of study, you are expected to use the cases like basic building blocks which you are then required to put together to erect a structure (the law for that particular subject). When you start out, however, you really don't comprehend what the "block" is all about and you can't visualize what the "building" is supposed to look like. Even after you finish the course, you have only a hazy outline of what should by that time be clear as an architect's best rendering. Most law students spend the week just before exams struggling to get that clear picture, a lot don't succeed—it's too late.

The time spent studying the table of contents of the casebook gives you some idea right from the beginning of what goal you are striving toward. Over the following weeks, as you progress, the image becomes clearer. When finals approach, you can spend your time studying a sharp, professional-looking picture instead of trying to stretch a hastily sketched drawing into a well-crafted watercolor painting.

During the four weeks before school starts, you should do your utmost to get at least three weeks ahead of the assignment schedule in terms of class preparation. The more ahead you can get, the better you'll be. If you keep that lead throughout the semester, you'll have plenty of time to study for finals without the tremendous pressure of trying to do class work and study for exams at the same time.

Incidentally, this is as good a time as any to let you know that, if you're taking a regular three-year day school program, and you want to get through with the knowledge and good grades that will give you the confidence you should have to pass the bar examination, you've got to figure on at least sixty hours of work every week.

Most students eventually get into small study groups and go over the material as the courses progress. This is a good idea—but I suggest that first you learn the material alone, before you go to the group meeting, so you get a solid base and will be able to recognize the errors of the others.

The give and take of bull sessions when discussing the application of the law you're learning to hypothetical situations is an important part of your training. But if you are the member of the group who can best explain difficult material to the others, you'll get the most out of it.

One important thing to keep in mind is that you will only get out of law school what you put into it. And the more solid your law school base, the better lawyer you'll be in later years.

6
HOW TO STUDY FOR CLASS

In most law school classes, the professor will call on a student to "give the case." This means that the student should tell how the case comes up on appeal, state the facts, give the issue involved, and state the rule. The ensuing class discussion will concern itself with the application of the rule to other facts, always similar, but slightly different from the main case you started out with.

When the professor asks you to "give the case," you should present your "brief" of it. In preparing the work, most students will read the case only twice, once to get some idea of it, and then a second time as they laboriously go through, underlining certain phrases in the text, and then writing down something or other to read back in class. It takes anywhere from thirty to sixty minutes to do this. And later, when they try to remember what they have done, they're lost.

Keep in mind that the cases you read in law school are the appellate decisions of the trial court cases which have been appealed by the losing party. The trial court has determined the facts. The appellate court is generally limited to those facts and does not reach an independent conclusion as to what they are.

An appeal is like a box. If the facts are not in the box, the appellate court can't get to them. The appellate court does not take any evidence. It is bound by the record sent up to it by the court below. Accordingly, the appellate court has to take the facts presented to it as true.

Frequently, law students are troubled because they worry about how the court *knows* these facts are true. Since the trial court record is all the appellate court has to go on, it normally doesn't concern itself with how the facts that come before it were established. The appellate court in effect says: Given the following set of facts, this is what we believe the law is in relation to those facts.

So how do you prepare for class? Obviously, you have to *read* the case first. But most students try to *write* the case. What do I mean? Literally, I mean "write." With ready pencil, they start to read; but as they read, they immediately underline and write down what they think may be important. Then, after one reading, they try to understand what they think they have read. Under my method, you'll spend the same thirty to sixty minutes they do, *but instead of reading the case twice and writing it down once, you'll actually read it about fifteen times and not write down anything at all.*

The first and most important thing to do, therefore, is: PUT YOUR PENCIL DOWN! *Just read. As fast as you can.* First, read the case over five or six times. Use your law dictionary on the first reading as necessary. Get the feel of the case. What are the facts? Who's involved? What are they fighting about? Always remember that, unless you have a controversy, you don't have a lawsuit.

Now, start reading more slowly. Keep the facts in mind. Look at the rule of the case that you copied from the textbook. It's at the top of the page. See how the case came up on appeal. Read the case five or six times more and see if you can understand the reasoning of the court which caused it to formulate the rule. Keep reading until you really understand it. Finally, when you think you have it all in your mind, read it over again a couple of times to solidify your conception.

Remember, *under this method, you don't read the case to find out what the rule is; you read it, knowing the rule (because it's up at the top of the page), to find out how the court logically concluded what the rule is—how the case logically is the next step in the development of the total structure which is the law of the subject you are studying.*

The basic idea is to spend as much time reading and as little writing as possible. In the time it would take to write everything out, you will have read the case in depth numerous times.

If you use my method, you *must* read the case many times. Don't shortchange yourself on this aspect. You have to spend as much time reading as you would if you had followed the customary method.

As you do this repetitive reading, you will find that the points in the case start jumping off the page at you. You'll see things and understand phrases you wouldn't believe possible. And when you get to class, you'll be so familiar with the case that you'll literally know as much about it as the professor. At the very least, you'll be one of the few students in the class who can intelligently discuss it with him.

When you finally feel that you have the case down solidly, you are ready to use your pencil. But all you do is put something in the margin of the casebook. That should be your primary memo pad. Guess what you put down. Words? No. Funny little pictures. I don't mean doodling. I'm not kidding. You draw pictures. Simple kindergarten stick figures that will help you have total and instant recall for a long time to come. You don't have to have any artistic ability whatever.

Let's look at a real case taken from the official Massachusetts reports. It's the kind that might be in any casebook on torts. Here's how Judge Knowlton wrote the opinion for the court. (The "J." after "Knowlton" stands for "Judge." It's not his initial.)

BOOTH v. MERRIAM *et al*
Supreme Judicial Court of Massachusetts
(1892) 155 Mass. 521

TORT, for personal injuries occasioned to the plaintiff by falling into a cesspool upon land of the defendants, negligently suffered by them to be out of repair.

At the trial in the Superior Court, before *Mason*, C. J., there was evidence tending to show that the defendants were the owners of the house numbered 29 on Harvard Street in Boston, which set back from the street fifty or sixty feet, and of a yard in front of the house, and also another yard in the rear of the house; that the plaintiff's son, acting for his mother, hired the house of the defendants' agent, by a parol lease at a monthly rent, about three months before the time of said accident, and the plaintiff had lived therein for these three months, carrying on the business of keeping boarders; that when the house was hired nothing was said about any yard, either in front or in the rear of the same; that the front yard was used to gain access to the house, and also to three or four other houses; that the yard in the rear was apparently designed only to be used by those occupying said house No. 29; that the cesspool was situated in the yard back of the house, and was used as a receptacle of the water that ran from the sink in the house, and was covered by a wooden frame, into which was set an iron cover; that the plaintiff, on the day of the accident, went out of the back door of said house, and started to go to a tub, which was placed under a window at the rear of said house, for the purpose of putting a piece of meat under the tub, this being where the plaintiff kept her meat; and that in walking from the back door towards the tub she stepped upon the iron cover, which was on a level with the surface of the ground, when it suddenly fell, causing the plaintiff to fall into the cesspool, and injuring her severely. The evidence tended to show that the plaintiff did not know anything about the location of the cesspool, nor the manner in which it was covered, and that she did not notice anything about it at the time; that the wooden frame in which the iron cover was placed had become so badly decayed as to be incapable of holding any weight; and the plaintiff contended, upon the evidence, that it must have been in the same condition at the time when said house was hired as aforesaid. No question was made that the plaintiff did not exercise due care.

Upon the above evidence, the judge ruled that the defendants would not be liable to the plaintiff in this action, and that the action could not be maintained.

The jury returned a verdict for the defendants; and the plaintiff alleged exceptions.

KNOWLTON, J. In an ordinary lease of a dwelling-house there is no implied covenant that the premises are in good repair or fit for habitation. "The rule of *caveat emptor* applies, and it is for the lessee to make the examination necessary to determine whether the premises he hires are safe, and adapted to the purposes for which they are hired." *Cowen* v. *Sunderland,* 145 Mass. 363. *Stevens* v. *Pierce,* 151 Mass. 207. If there is a concealed defect that renders the premises dangerous which the tenant cannot discover by the exercise of reasonable diligence, of which the landlord has or ought to have knowledge, it is the landlord's duty to disclose it, and he is liable for an injury which results from his concealment of it. *Cowen* v. *Sunderland, ubi supra. Minor* v. *Sharon,* 112 Mass. 477. *Bowe* v. *Hunking,* 135 Mass. 380. *Martin* v. *Richards, ante,* 381.

The plaintiff contends that this case shows the existence of such a defect, and that it is like *Cowen* v. *Sunderland,* in which it appeared that there was a cesspool covered with decayed boards and earth four to six inches deep, on which grass and weeds were growing, in a yard hired by the plaintiff, and that it had been repaired with old boards some time before by the defendant's direction. The case at bar differs from that in important particulars. There was an iron cover set in a wooden frame which covered the cesspool, and was level with the surface of the ground, thereby disclosing to everybody that there was a covered excavation there designed for use. The accident happened solely because the frame was old and out of repair, and there is nothing to show that its condition was not easily discoverable on examination, or that the defendant had actual knowledge of its condition, or was culpably responsible for it. It was as much the duty of the plaintiff, when she hired the house and yard, to examine the premises and ascertain whether they were in such repair that she could safely use them, as of the defendant. The case is similar to *Bowe* v. *Hunking, ubi supra,* and it falls within the general rule that a tenant cannot recover for an injury received by reason of the want of repair of the premises hired.   *Exceptions overruled.*

During the first four weeks prior to the beginning of the semester, you would have looked up this case in a tort textbook and would have written the rule of the case across the top of the page above the heading, BOOTH v. MERRIAM *et al.*: A LANDLORD IS NOT LIABLE TO THE TENANT FOR OBVIOUS DEFECTS IN THE PREMISES.

Keeping that rule in mind, and pretending that you actually are getting ready for the first semester in law school, let's see how the method of study I've proposed will work for you.

Read *Booth* v. *Merriam* four or five times quickly. See if you can get the "feel" of this case. Who's fighting? What's the argument about? Why is this case up on appeal, anyway? Why is it in your casebook?

What have we discovered? Elizabeth Booth has rented a house from George Merriam. Out in the back yard is a cesspool. It has an iron cover set in a wooden frame. It's readily identifiable. It's even with the ground. Any reasonable person can observe that the wooden frame is old and rotten. Nevertheless, our dear Elizabeth walks on the cover and, wonder of wonders, the frame gives way and she falls into the cesspool, right up to her neck.

Now she's suing Merriam for damages: physical injuries, medical expenses, pain and suffering.

The trial court ruled in favor of Merriam. Elizabeth's lawyer entered an "exception" to the ruling to technically preserve her right to appeal.

Now the case is before the high court of the state. The issue is whether a landlord is liable to a tenant for injuries received because of an obvious defect in the premises. In the decision which you have just read, the court answered that question in the negative, setting forth its reasons for its conclusion. So, we have the rule of the case which you wrote at the top of the page.

Since you've reached this point in your thinking, keep testing the method of study. Read the case over, slowly this time, at least ten times. Read it until you actually feel that you know why each word is there. Read it until you are certain you understand how the court logically applied the rule to the specific facts of this case. Note how a slightly different set of facts did not fit by analogy and how a different rule was reached in that situation. Is it clear to you why the rule in *Cowen* v. *Sunderland* is not applicable here? Do you see that this case is a developmental step in this area of the law?

As an experiment, see how well you can explain this case to someone else. Then, let them read it and see what they get out of it. You'll find that even with your clear explanation, they will have a lot more difficulty than you did, because of your intimate knowledge of the case, the result of the many times you went over it to prepare for this experiment. You will feel extremely secure in your analysis because you will have absorbed practically every piece of relevant information that could be found in the case.

Try drawing a simple stick figure that will help you remember this case. With the multiple reading of it you have done, plus the picture, you'll probably never forget it, or the rule and the reasoning behind it.

You may find it helpful to make an analytical diagram of the case to get you over some of the tough thought processes if you run into any trouble understanding what is happening. Here's a possibility for this case:

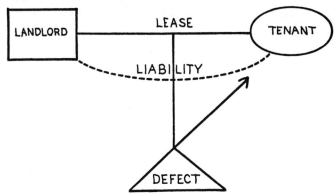

A word of caution. Just because this case is in your casebook doesn't mean that it necessarily is the law today. It has been put in to show you the developmental history of the law. Some states may still use the rule. Others may have originally come to an opposite decision. The rule may be completely changed by statute, or a more modern tenant-oriented court may have overruled an old decision in its jurisdiction. The law is flexible and changes from time to time. But this case represents the rule at common law.

7
IT ALL COMES FROM THE COMMON LAW

In England, there were two kinds of law right from the beginning of the court system: the statutes enacted by Parliament, and the opinions of the judges found in the cases (the common law). That broad distinction carries over into American law, with the added difference that the common law of the United States includes all the law of England, both statutory and common law, as it existed when independence was declared on July 4, 1776. Although the term is not used too much, the common law of the United States also consists of the judicial decisions of the several state courts. It does not include the enactments of Congress and the various state legislatures.

What you learn in law school, in the main, is the common law. That's what the bar examiners in most of the states examine you on. But in each state, the examination also includes material considered pertinent to practice in that state. Thus, in California, you are examined on the law of community property. And practically every state examines on its own rules of evidence, practice and procedure.

Many students wonder whether it's really important to know the common law today when the statutes have codified so many areas. Yes, it is. Even though, for example, a state statute may specifically say there is no common law crime in that state, on occasion the court must go to the common law to interpret statutes.

When I was a deputy attorney general handling prosecution appeals, I once used the common law to suggest over-ruling a criminal conviction because the trial court result seemed unjust. The court didn't say so, but ancient common law was the basis of the decision. At common law, it was no crime to take food from an innkeeper without paying. It was only after a special innkeepers' statute was passed by Parliament that it became the crime of "defrauding an innkeeper."

Here, the defendant and two associates went into an all-night restaurant, ordered steak and eggs, and tried to get out the back window without paying. The chef met them with a meat cleaver. The two associates pled guilty to petty theft and each paid twenty-five-dollar fines. The defendant had a prior felony conviction, so he went to prison. Petty theft with a prior conviction is a felony in California.

This is what the decision looked like before publication in 226 Cal. App. 2d 305 (1964):

IN THE DISTRICT COURT OF APPEAL
OF THE STATE OF CALIFORNIA
SECOND APPELLATE DISTRICT
DIVISION FOUR

THE PEOPLE,
    Plaintiff and Respondent

           v.

VERNON EARL FIENE,
    Defendant and Appellant.

2d Crim 9225
FILED
April 18, 1964

APPEAL from a judgment of the Superior Court of Los Angeles County. Joseph L. Call, Judge. Reversed.

Prosecution for petty theft with a prior conviction of a felony. Judgment of conviction reversed.

Defendant was found guilty by the court of a violation of section 667 of the Penal Code, petty theft with a prior conviction of a felony. Probation was denied and defendant was sentenced to a county jail term. He appeals from the judgment of conviction. A résumé of the facts is as follows:

On February 11, 1963 at about 3:00 A.M., defendant and two other men entered the Valley-Ho restaurant and ordered meals. After eating, defendant got up, went to the restroom for a few minutes, and then left the restaurant by the side exit. One of the two remaining men asked for and was given the check for the price of the meals. Approximately ten minutes after defendant had left, the other two men started for the restroom, and then left by the same exit defendant had used. No one paid the check in the amount of about eight dollars. The manager saw the two men leave and followed them outside. When he yelled at them, one of the men took off running. He then saw defendant standing behind a station wagon in the parking lot. When he shouted to some of his customers, who had emerged from the restaurant, asking that they get the police, defendant and the other man also ran off.

Two or three weeks prior to this episode a similar incident took place at the same restaurant. Defendant and the first man to run, had come in, ordered meals and left without paying for them. On that occasion, after eating, defendant went to the restroom, the other man followed shortly thereafter, and then both left by the same side exit.

Defendant told an investigating police officer, who spoke to him at his home on the morning of the February 11 incident, that he had been home all night. However, he later told the same officer that he had been to the restaurant with the other two men; there had been no agreement as to who would pay; after eating he went to the restroom; he then left and walked home.

Defendant stated to another police officer that he had been drinking before he entered the restaurant; at the time he entered he had only 25 cents on his person; the first man who had run, Weeder, was going to pay the check. When the officer later told defendant he had talked with Weeder, and Weeder denied even being in the restaurant that morning, defendant said, "Well, it wasn't Weeder that was going to pay the check. Some fellow in the next booth was going to pay. I don't know who he was." Defendant then said he had never seen the man in the next booth before.

At the trial, the People introduced records showing that defendant had two prior felony convictions and that he had served state prison terms as a result of each.

We find no merit in the sole contention raised by defendant, namely that the evidence is insufficient to sustain the verdict. The rules declared in *People* v. *Newland*, 15 Cal. 2d 678, require that we make such a finding. However, the attorney general, with commendable objectivity, raises a much more serious question, one which is raised for the first time in these proceedings, and, one which, we believe, requires a reversal of the judgment.

The question presented is whether the existence of Penal Code section 537 (The Innkeeper Statute), making it a misdemeanor to defraud an innkeeper, prevents the superior court from acquiring jurisdiction in this matter.

Section 537 reads in part: "Any person who obtains any food . . . at an hotel, inn, restaurant, . . . without paying thereof, with intent to defraud the proprietor or manager thereof, . . . is guilty of a misdemeanor." Defendant was charged with and convicted of the crime of petty theft with a prior conviction of a felony. (Pen. Code, §667.) Section 484 of the Penal Code is the general statute defining theft. The value of the property taken in the instant case was well under the $200 limit for petty theft.

The rule is well established that where a general statute, standing alone, includes the same matter as a special statute, and thus conflicts with it, the special act is to be considered as an exception to the general statute, whether it was passed before or after the general enactment. (*In re Williamson*, 43 Cal. 2d 651, 654; *People* v. *Swann*, 213 Cal. App. 2d 447, 449.)

The attorney general, in raising this issue, concedes that the elements of the special statute making it a crime to defraud an innkeeper (§537), are the same as the elements of petty theft, but nevertheless maintains, that the above stated rule should not be applicable in this case. It is argued that the legislature did not intend that section 537 should be applicable where, as here, the defendant could be prosecuted under another statute providing a greater penalty. The legislature, the attorney general asserts, "would not want to give less protection to . . . innkeepers and restaurant proprietors if the defrauding was carried out by a released felon." No authority has been cited, however, in support of such an interpretation.

In the case of *In re Joiner*, 180 Cal. App. 2d 250, the defendant, after taking his automobile to a garage for repairs, later entered the premises of the garage after closing hours, and, without permission, retook possession of the automobile. He was subsequently apprehended and charged with burglary and grand theft. The appellate court, relying on the rule stated in the case of *In re Williamson, supra,* held that the superior court was without subject matter jurisdiction to try defendant because his conduct came within the provisions of a special statute, section 430 of the Vehicle Code (now Civ. Code, §3075, and formerly Pen. Code, §537[d]), making it a misdemeanor for anyone by trick or device to take a vehicle held subject to a lien. (See also the recent case of *People* v. *Swann, supra,* decided by this court, wherein upon similar facts, the same rule was applied.) We feel that these cases are determinative in the instant case.

The judgment of conviction is reversed.

JEFFERSON, J.

We concur:
 BURKE, P. J.
 KINGSLEY, J.

I've set out the case at length so you'll have another opportunity to see what a case in your casebook might look like if you are actually in law school.

You'll see another example where the common law was very important when we get to the chapter on appellate briefing.

The basic reason for teaching the common law in law schools is so that you will have some idea as to how law developed and you will use that historic logic pattern to develop new theories of law to apply to current situations.

8

WRESTLING AROUND WITH THE WRITS

From almost the first day of law school you'll hear about "writs." The writ was the first document filed in a lawsuit at common law. It was issued to a prospective plaintiff, for a fee, by one of the king's officials. The writ contained the names of the parties, a description of what the contention was, and a direction to a sheriff to serve it on the defendant and bring him into court.

The history of writs starts in 1066 A.D. That's the big date in English law. In that year, King William of Normandy established his legal right to the English throne by triumphing over King Harold at the Battle of Hastings. After the victory, William divided the kingdom among his supporters and introduced a method of government known as the feudal system.

Feudalism was based on land ownership. Everyone in the kingdom owed allegiance to the king through the land-owner directly above. Serfs, a cut above slaves, were bound to the land where they were born and their allegiance was to the lord of their manor. The landowner's allegiance was to the noble directly over him and that noble's allegiance was also to the noble above him, and so on.

The centralization of allegiance brought strong centralization of government. Laws operative throughout the realm were proclaimed in the king's name. Taxes were collected and funneled into the central treasury. A system of royal courts evolved for the settlement of disputes between subjects in civil matters, and for the settlement of criminal disputes between king and subject in criminal matters.

Initially, the judicial structure was totally located at the seat of government and was literally "the king's court." Cases were heard before the king and the assembled nobles, and the king, acting as judge, decided the results after discussion with the nobles.

With the progression of time and the growing volume of business, the king gradually referred the cases to his chancellor for determination.

A bureaucracy rapidly developed in the chancellor's offices (chancery) as it became necessary to screen the requests for hearing to determine what kind of case it was, what was necessary to give the defendant an opportunity to present the other side, how much time would it take, etc. After the details were determined, a writ was composed and the case commenced.

Eventually, the litigants throughout the kingdom persuaded the king to establish a system of branch courts. Members of the chancellor's staff were appointed judges and went out on circuit to hear cases in the provinces. A group of expert lawyers gradually developed to handle the cases presented before the courts.

William Blackstone, the great early English law writer, gives an excellent description of the court structure, the bar, and the various types of cases in his monumental treatise, *Commentaries on the Laws of England.* Browse through all four volumes at the earliest opportunity. Not only will you obtain some good background on the court structure, but you will be exposed to an in-depth discussion of much of the law school work in pleading, property, contracts, torts, and crimes. When you are actually studying these subjects in class, you will know where to look in Blackstone to find an explanation for some difficult point.

Incidentally, after you are in law school a while—don't do it now because you won't get too much out of it until you know what to look for—be sure to get a stack pass from the librarian and spend some time rummaging through the older books on the shelves. You'll find that such exploratory reading will not only broaden your legal understanding, but will make you aware of social customs and practices which you never suspected existed so many years ago.

The spread of the court system led to the proliferation of writs covering every type of controversy. To make their jobs easier, the writ clerks persuaded the chancellor to establish a rule that no new writs would be issued, that in order to get into court it was necessary that the facts of the case fit one of the writs used in the past.

Most of these old writs are described in the law dictionaries. Here are a couple found in Blacks to give you some idea of what they were and how they fit into the legal system. You'll probably never hear of these in law school; however, they did exist.

Let's look at a hypothetical situation applied to a real writ.

De pipa vini carianda was a writ which described the situation where a wine seller had engaged a person to transport his wine to a tavern in an adjacent town. On the way, if the "pipe," or container, broke, the seller sued the carrier.

Because this writ had successfully stood up in court, and because the seller won his case, the writ was added to the list of known writs which could be used. If you could get a set of facts within the original language of four corners of the writ, you could bring your case. If you couldn't, you were out of court.

Under the system then in effect, you could get into court and get legal redress only if your factual situation were covered by a known writ. At the present time, under modern pleading, the attorney looks at the facts and then draws his complaint to fit them.

Let's suppose for a minute that six friends went into a tavern in those days, sat at a big, rough, oaken table in the back near the fireplace, and ordered a round of drinks; then another, and another.

In this place, the proprietor put a big jug of wine on the table. As the friends drank, they poured their own. The proprietor charged them by the glass—he observed and noted with a charcoal mark over the fireplace each time a glass was filled.

In the revelry, one of the friends dropped the container; the big jug cracked and the joy-filling contents were transformed into a mournful stain on the floor. The proprietor demanded that the friends pay for the undrunk beverage at what he estimated was the per-glass rate. They refused. He sued.

His lawyer couldn't find any writ to cover this kind of case. But perhaps a colleague in the profession remembered that in another shire, or county, a writ of *de pipa vini carianda* had successfully been brought some years previously.

The old file copy of the writ was obtained, names were changed, and the lawyer argued that breaking a jug at a table when you didn't own it or the contents was the same as breaking it in transit when you were delivering it from maker to tavern owner.

If the court hearing the case agreed with the analogy, the writ would be granted. However, in this hypothetical case, the strict construction prevalent at that time undoubtedly would have resulted in a verdict for the defense. The facts did not fit the writ.

When you study Real Property and Future Interests, among your other law school subjects, you'll find that the English system of land titles was extremely complex. It became very important when a man died that his heirs be known with certainty.

Every once in a while some enterprising widow would claim to be pregnant in order to suggest the possibility that there was an unborn heir in existence who might take the estate. They had a writ for that situation, too. *De ventre inspicienda* was a court order to permit knowledgeable persons to examine the widow to determine if she were actually "with child."

This writ always reminds me of the story about the elderly scrivener (deed-drawer) whose occupation made him very precise with words. Once, while he was on a vacation through the northern farm country, he stopped at a little inn for a mid-morning snack. The menu delighted him. One of his favorite dishes was on it—strawberries and cream. Thinking of big, red-whiskered strawberries piled high in a bowl, and another bowl of freshly drawn cream in which he could individually dip each succulent strawberry, he gave the waitress his order: "Strawberries *and* cream, please."

A little later, to his great dismay, she placed a bowl of cream before him in which were dumped the strawberries he had hoped to gently dip one by one. He chastised the waitress.

"My good woman. I ordered strawberries *and* cream. You brought strawberries *with* cream."

"What's the difference, eh? One's the same as the other."

"It definitely is *not*. I hope that someday you will never have to learn the difference between a woman *and* child and a woman *with* child."

The prohibition on issuance of new writs eventually reached a compromise. The lawyers got the law changed, and about eleven writs came to be used most of the time. These covered almost every situation. The eleven writs developed into what was known as "causes of action." In order to have a cause of action, the factual situation had to conform to certain principles, different for each type of cause. These principles became known as the "elements of a cause of action."

Here's a list of the eleven common law causes of action:

COVENANT: Action brought when a defendant failed to perform a contract under seal (a contract formalized by signature and a seal impressed in wax).

INDEBITATUS ASSUMPSIT: Action on an oral or written contract, not under seal, where the broken promise is implied from the terms of the contract.

SPECIAL ASSUMPSIT: Action on a contract, not under seal, where the defendant has breached a specific promise in the contract.

DEBT: Action to recover a specific sum of money, the amount being readily ascertainable.

TROVER: Action for damages where someone has unlawfully taken another's personal property.

REPLEVIN: Action to recover the personal property itself which was unlawfully taken.

DETINUE: Action to recover personal property originally rightfully possessed, but not returned when due, together with damages for the unlawful keeping.

ACCOUNT: Action on the balance of a series of transactions between the parties (sometimes called "common counts").

EJECTMENT: Action for recovery of land, together with damages for the unlawful possession.

TRESPASS: Action for damages for direct injury to the plaintiff.

TRESPASS ON THE CASE: Action for damages for indirect injury to the plaintiff (often referred to as "case").

While modern pleading does not use these divisions of causes of actions, it is still necessary to be familiar with them in order to comprehend the present-day philosophy relating to the elements of a cause of action. If the plaintiff fails to prove every essential element of the case, the case is lost.

9
THE PAPERS IN THE OLDER CASES

In order to give you background for modern law, you will be exposed to a number of old cases, particularly those which established landmarks in the law. Without at least a rudimentary knowledge of the papers filed at the trial court level in the old days, you may get quite confused, for frequently the old decisions confuse procedure and substance in their analyses.

As we noted in the last chapter, the first document issued was the writ. It was generally lengthy, and served two functions. It set out the ultimate facts of the plaintiff's complaint, and also directed the sheriff to serve it on the defendant and bring him before the court. To the writ was attached the plaintiff's declaration, which detailed the elements of the cause of action.

Here's what a writ of trespass for assault and battery looked like. This one is taken from *A Treatise on the Principles of Pleading in Civil Actions* by Henry John Stephen, published by Robert H. Small of Philadelphia in 1831. It is typical of the writs of trespass used for hundreds of years.

George the Fourth, by the Grace of God, of the United Kingdom of Great Britain and Ireland, King, Defender of the Faith, to the Sheriff of Nottingham, greeting. *If Albert Bottom shall make you secure of prosecuting his claim, then put by gages and safe pledges, Charles Dawson,* late of Kentbury, yeoman, *that he be before us on the morrow of All Souls, wheresoever we shall then be in Eng-*

land, *to show wherefore, with force and arms,* at Kentbury aforesaid, *he made an assault upon the said Albert Bottom and beat, wounded, and ill-treated him, so that his life was despaired of, and other wrongs to him then there did, to the damage of the said Albert Bottom, and against our peace;* and have you there the names of the pledges and this writ. Witness ourself, at Westminster, the 14th day of April in the 3rd year of our reign.

Signed, etc.

Stephen, *supra,* at page 15.

And just so you'll have a complete picture, here's what the declaration in the same case looked like:

In the King's Bench.

All Souls Term, in the 3rd year of the reign of King George the Fourth.

On August 4, 1823 to wit, *Charles Dawson was attached to answer Albert Bottom of a plea, wherefore he the said Charles Dawson with force and arms, at Kentbury in the County of Nottingham made an assault upon the said Albert Bottom and beat, wounded and ill-treated him, so that his life was despaired of, and other wrongs to him there did, to the damage of said Albert Bottom and against the peace of our Lord the now King. And thereupon the said Albert Bottom,* by Warren Tompson his attorney, *complains:* For that the *said Charles Dawson* heretofore, to wit, on the fourth day of April in the year of our Lord One Thousand Eight Hundred and Twenty-three, *with force and arms,* at Kentbury aforesaid, in the county aforesaid, *made an assault upon the said Albert Bottom,* and then and there beat, wounded and ill-treated him, so that his life was despaired of, and other wrongs to the said Albert Bottom then and there did; against the peace of our said Lord the King, and *to the damage of the said Albert Bottom of One Thousand Pounds,* 1000 £.; and therefore he brings his suit, wherefore he prays judgment, and his damages by him sustained, by reason of the committing of said trespasses, to be adjudged to him.

Signed, etc.

Stephen, *supra,* at page 46.

The defendant had to reply to the writ and declaration. But first, it was necessary to put up security for costs (the "gages" and "pledges" mentioned in the writ, above) with the sheriff and agree to appear at the time directed. Failure to do so meant arrest and confinement. On the other hand, if a plaintiff lost a case and couldn't pay the defendant's costs, the plaintiff was arrested. Here's an interesting entry from the record of the court of chancery in the sixteenth century which I came across while browsing through Monro's *Acta Cancellariae,* published by William Benning and Co. of London in 1847. (Don't let the fancy title throw you—the whole book is printed in English.)

Geldard v. Gardyner, 12 Feb. 1596.

Forasmuch *as the plaintiff is so poor, that he is not able to pay the costs* for an insufficient bill [a declaration which failed to state a cause of action when tested in court] for which an attachment went forth against him, *and therefore was appointed to be whipped; and for that, instead of whipping, the said plaintiff hath stood upon the pillory;* it is ordered by the Lord Keeper that the costs and the said contempt be clearly discharged, and that a Supersedes as be awarded for that purpose; but *if he vex any more in this sort in forma pauperis* [the courthad granted him permission to sue without putting up any fees because he was a pauper], *then he shall, at the next time, be whipped.*

Monro, *supra,* at page 690.

Occasionally, the courts showed greater compassion, as Monro indicates with this order issued in *Danyell v. Jackson,* November 17, 1575:

Whereas the matter in variance between the said parties was, the 5th of this month, dismissed for such causes as are in the said order expressed, and the plaintiff adjudged thereby to pay the defendant 30s. costs; forasmuch as *the plaintiff being a very poor boy, in very simple clothes and bare-legged, and under the age of twelve years, came this present day into this Court, and desired that he might be discharged of his said costs;* it is, therefore, *in consideration, as well of his age, as also of his poverty and simplicity,* ORDERED THAT (upon an affidavit made that he is the same Laurence Danyell named plaintiff herein) *he be discharged of the said 30s. costs,* and no process to issue out against him for the same.

Monro, *supra,* at page 433.

In response to the writ and declaration filed by the plaintiff, the defendant had several options. He could deny the allegations in a "traverse" and plead what was known as "the general issue"—"throwing himself on the country" (asking for a jury trial)—or he could respond by making a technical objection to the declaration in the form of a "demurrer," a "plea in abatement," or a "plea in bar."

You'll get into these in some depth in your first year of law school. The demurrer admitted the facts alleged in the declaration to be true, but argued that the declaration nevertheless failed to state a cause of action. Other pleas might be that the plaintiff lacked legal capacity to sue or that there was a similar action then pending between the same parties.

If the defendant's technical objection was upheld, the plaintiff had to file a second pleading and the process was repeated. Eventually, the various pleadings resulted in an issue being reached on which the case was tried.

The lineup of the pleadings looked like this:

Plaintiff	*Defendant*
Writ and declaration	Plea of General Issue (Traverse), or demurrer, or other technical plea
Replication	Rejoinder
Surrejoinder	Rebutter
Surrebutter	

Inasmuch as the purpose of common law pleading was either to reach an issue of law which the court could decide based on admitted facts, or an issue of fact which the court could decide based on applicable law, the subsequent pleadings after the declaration and demurrer normally got shorter and shorter. Most of the cases never got further than the replication stage.

Accordingly, the judges got rather testy if a lawyer made the pleadings too lengthy or padded them with scurrilous allegations. Monro cites several cases where verbose and libelous pleaders were rigidly disciplined to teach them not to repeat their performances. *Mylward* v. *Weldon*, February 15, 1596, is one of the most interesting and unusual ones:

Forasmuch as it now appeared to this Court, by a report made by the now Lord Keeper (being then Master of the Rolls), upon consideration had of the plaintiff's replication, . . . *that the said replication doth amount to six score sheets of paper, and yet all the matter thereof which is pertinent might have been well contrived in sixteen sheets of paper,* wherefore the plaintiff was appointed to be examined to find out who drew the same replication, and by whose advice it was done, to the end that the offender might, for example sake, not only be punished, but also be fined to Her Majesty for that offence; and that the defendant might have his charges sustained thereby; . . . *and for that it now appeared to His Lordship, by the confession of Richard Mylward, alias Alexander, the plaintiff's son, that he the said Richard himself, did both draw, devise, and engross the same replication;* and because His Lordship is of the opinion that *such an abuse is not to be tolerated,* proceeding of a malicious purpose to increase the defendant's charge, and being fraught with much impertinent matter not fit for this Court; *it is therefore ordered, that the Warden of the Fleet shall take the said Richard Mylward, alias Alexander, into his custody, and shall bring him into Westminster Hall,* on Saturday next, about ten of the clock in the forenoon, *and then and there shall cut a hole in the myddest of the same engrossed replication* (which is delivered unto him for that purpose) *and put the said Richard's head through the same hole, and so let the same replication hang about his shoulders, with the written side outward; and then, the same so hanging, shall lead the same Richard, bare headed and bare faced, round about Westminster Hall, whilst the Courts are sitting, and shall show him at the bar of every one of the three Courts within the Hall,* and shall take him back again to the Fleet, and keep him prisoner, until he shall have paid 10 £. to Her Majesty for a fine, and 20 nobles to the defendant, for his costs in respect of the aforesaid abuse, which fine and costs are now adjudged and imposed upon him by this Court, for the abuse aforesaid.

Monro, *supra,* at page 692.

Besides the common law, there was another body of law which grew up called *equity.* Equity stepped in where law left off. Where money damages were inadequate as a remedy, equity could act. Thus, if one individual illegally drained waters over another's land, law could give money damages for the unlawful act. Equity, however, could issue an order to actually stop the improper drainage and to prevent it from happening again in the future. Noncompliance would result in imprisonment for contempt of court.

Equity courts were under the jurisdiction of the king's chancellor. They were called courts of chancery. Instead of calling the parties "plaintiff" and "defendant," they were referred to as "petitioner" and "respondent."

With the development of code pleading, both law and equity were frequently joined into one court system, and today, in most American jurisdictions, the county trial court can usually give whatever remedy is adequate and necessary under the facts presented.

But again, like the common law, it is still necessary to have a knowledge of the basic principles of equity even though the specialized practice of the subject no longer exists.

10
JUSTICE WITHOUT JURIES

When the word *trial* is mentioned today, most of us conjure up the picture of a courtroom with a judge sitting on the bench and twelve jurors sitting in the box deciding who will win the case.

The judge's function under modern law, besides the obvious one of presiding, is to make all necessary rulings on what the applicable law is, whereas the jury's duty is limited to determining what the facts are in the matter. If a jury has been waived by the parties, the judge takes over both facets of the trial.

Ruling on law includes determining questions of validity of pleadings (the papers filed by each side, i.e., complaint, demurrer, answer, etc.), admissibility of evidence, and propriety of questions asked witnesses by the lawyers; ruling on motions; and giving instructions to the jury so that they understand their function and know how to perform their duties. Most people who have served on juries don't realize that the lawyers draw up proposed instructions, and after a conference with these lawyers, the judge decides which instructions to give.

Determination of facts is done by evaluation of testimony of witnesses and analysis of evidence presented.

Great care is taken when a jury is picked to make sure that the jurors have no knowledge of either the parties or the facts of the case. If the judge has any connection with the parties or the lawyers, either by relationship or business dealings, he or she must disqualify him or herself and have another judge assigned to preside over the matter. The basic idea is to remove any possible bias or prejudice from the trial.

This was not always the way things were done. In the very early days of the common law there were two types of trials: trial by ordeal and trial by oath or compurgators.

Trial by ordeal was based on religious and superstitious beliefs originating in tribal practices of days not long past. It's a little hard for us to realize that, before the Norman conquest in 1066, what is now England was primarily made up of many little tribes, each controlling its own localized territory. Their antecedents went back to ancient Norse and Germanic societies—Vikings, Danes, Angles, Saxons, Jutes—and customs continued for many years.

Trial by ordeal was used primarily in criminal cases. Testimony was given against the accused. Denial of commission of the crime was made. The factual issue was settled through some form of torture. If the accused survived, acquittal resulted. Blackstone describes this form of trial in the *Commentaries,* volume IV, chapter XXVII, page 342:

The most ancient species of trial was that by ordeal. . . . This was of two sorts, either *fire-ordeal, or water-ordeal;* the former being confined to persons of higher rank, the latter to the common people. *Both of these might be performed by a deputy;* but the principal was to answer for the success of the trial; the deputy only venturing some corporeal pain, for hire, or perhaps for friendship. *Fire-ordeal was performed either by taking up, in the hand, unhurt, a piece of red-hot iron, of one, two, or three pounds weight; or else by walking barefoot, and blindfold, over nine red-hot ploughshares, laid lengthwise at unequal distances: and if the party escaped being hurt, he was adjudged innocent; but if it happened otherwise, as without collusion it usually did, he was then condemned as guilty.* However, by the latter method queen Emma, the mother of Edward the Confessor, is mentioned to have cleared her character, when suspected of familiarity with Alwyn bishop of Winchester.

Water-ordeal was performed, either by plunging the bare arm up to the elbow in boiling water and escaping unhurt thereby; or by casting the person suspect into a river or pond of cold water; and if he floated therein without any action of swimming, it was deemed an evidence of his guilt; but if he sunk, he was acquitted.

The old colonial ducking stool which we all read about in grammar school was a vestige of this ancient practice.

In civil cases, one of the ancient forms of trial was trial by oath, also known as trial by wager of oath, or trial by compurgators. The defendant came into court and denied the charge (usually that he owed money) under oath. He brought with him eleven neighbors, called "compurgators," who swore that they believed him.

The Normans brought an interesting type of trial from the continent, "trial by wager of battel." Initially, the parties themselves battled hand to hand in front of the king and assembled dignitaries of the court. Later, the system was altered to permit first the defendant, and then the plaintiff, to have a substitute do the fighting for them.

Well-known knights hired themselves out as champions for litigants. Lawyers drew the pleadings; knights fought the "battel." Generally, this was hand to hand.

You are all familiar with the movie scenes where the king and his courtiers sit on a field and watch opposing knights fight each other. Occasionally, jousts of this nature were lawsuits being tried before the court.

The groups of knights who worked together were really the trial law firms of the day.

The overtones of this system still continue in England today, where lawyers called solicitors take care of the paperwork law, and lawyers called barristers actually go into court and try the cases.

It's fun to speculate that, perhaps, when the Blue Medallion Knights helped some beautiful golden-tressed maiden confined to an isolated ivory tower by her cruel guardian, they were really just lawyers taking a case on a contingency basis, and if they won at the jousts, the firm got a percentage of her estate and the junior partner married the girl he had so successfully championed.

I recall reading an article once which said that trial by combat was not really banned in England until the last part of the nineteenth century, when some clever litigant demanded that right. Before the case got to actual trial, however, Parliament hurriedly passed a statute limiting the form of all trials to judge, or judge and jury proceedings.

We probably get our twelve jurors from the defendant and eleven compurgators; the lawyers from the knights combatant, and the judges from first the king, then the judges he appointed to make the rounds of the kingdom on a more regular basis.

If you read something on the life of Abraham Lincoln you'll find that, in his day, the courts of the state went on periodic circuits with judge and lawyers traveling around to try the cases coming up for the term. And as you study your cases for this period, you'll find a number of them raise questions relating to the effects of events occurring during one term on a case tried at a later term. This was also true in the federal courts. Today, each United States Supreme Court justice is still considered the judge responsible for all matters in one of the appellate circuits.

Basically, the jury is a part of the "law," as contrasted with the "equity" side of the justice process. This was true from ancient days when "law" covered criminal prosecutions and suits for money damages. The jury determinations of the facts concluded the case. Keep in mind that, in any case where a jury trial is required, it may be waived if all parties agree (stipulate) to the waiver. On the equity side, a jury was not used unless the judge wanted it to make some factual determination for him. In those cases, however, the judge made the final determination of the result of the case. This is still true today. Equity matters are generally referred to as "proceedings."

Today, a judge sitting without a jury issues various writs ordering people to do or refrain from doing certain things. Probate of wills and administration of decedent estates, trusts, and guardianships are all nonjury proceedings. Bankruptcy is another.

One of the largest volume-generating nonjury areas is in the field of Administrative Law.

If Administrative Law is only an elective at your law school, be sure to take it. More and more, our daily lives are governed by the rules and regulations and decisions and determinations of administrative agencies.

A home owner wants to convert her garage into another bedroom. The local, county planning officer says she can't do it because of a particular interpretation of the zoning ordinance. Her appeals to the planning commission, and from there to the county board of supervisors are administrative proceedings. Hearings are held where evidence is taken, legal arguments are made, and a decision is issued.

A police captain in a large city refuses to issue a permit to carry a gun to a store owner in the precinct. He appeals to the Police Commission. Administrative proceeding.

The State Board of Cosmetology wants to revoke the license of a beauty shop because the combs are used on different customers without being sanitized before each new use. Administrative proceeding.

An airline wants a permit to fly a new route between two cities. It has to apply to the Federal Aviation Agency. Administrative proceeding.

Underlying all administrative proceedings is the basic theme that the officials and bureaucrats who have been delegated power by the legislative body of the federal government, a state, county, city, district, or other political entity, should not be allowed to reign unchecked in their power to regulate the activities within their control. The public protection against abuse is the administrative hearing and the appeal to the courts if the agency has abused its discretion and therefore acted illegally.

An administrative agency may consist of one person who makes the final decisions and the supporting staff, i.e., the Federal Bureau of Investigation; or a large group of people making up a board or commission, such as a State Board of Medical Examiners and its staff.

Administrative agencies usually have only that power which the legislative body has delegated to them. If they try to act in excess of that power, we say they have exceeded their jurisdiction.

These agencies customarily interpret this power granted to them by the legislative body through the issuance of regulations and rules governing their operations. Before these regulations or rules become final, an agency generally is required to give public notice of its intent to proclaim them and hold a hearing to allow for public input into the subjects under consideration. In the federal system and most states, petitions to prevent a regulation or rule from taking effect may be brought in court. A date will be set ordering the agency to refrain from effectuating the order or to "show cause" why it has not done so. The court will then hear legal arguments from both sides and issue its decision. This too is a nonjury proceeding.

If someone applies for a license and is turned down, or if the agency wants to revoke the license, a hearing is usually provided for. A hearing is always required if an agency wants to take away or interfere with some vested right. This hearing privilege may be waived by the person involved. The waiver can be express or by default. That is, the person can say, "I don't want one," or can fail to apply for one in the manner required by the statute or regulations.

Often, people will try to bypass some or all of the administrative procedures and go to court directly. They cannot do so. This is called the "doctrine of exhaustion of administrative remedies." The courts don't want to be cluttered up with a whole group of cases which really aren't final.

Let's suppose the holder of a physician's license is convicted of some crime involving illegal prescribing of narcotics. Under the procedure in this particular state, the secretary of the Board of Medical Examiners files an "Accusation" against the doctor before the Board, setting forth the charges and requesting that the license be revoked. The licensee files a denial.

The matter is set for hearing before a hearing officer or an Administrative Law judge. This individual may be employed by the Board or may be an independent hearing officer hired by the state.

After the hearing, the hearing officer makes a proposed decision which is submitted to the Board. The Board may accept it, in which case a decision is handed down. It is that final decision which is subject to appeal in the courts of the state. Administrative decisions are generally first appealed to the county court system rather than the state appellate courts.

If the Board does not like the decision, it may reject it. Under that circumstance it may rehear the case itself or may read a copy of the reporter's transcript and study the physical and documentary evidence introduced at the hearing. It can then send the case back to the hearing officer with instructions to take additional evidence or it may issue its final decision.

Because administrative proceedings may take quite some time, licensees will sometimes get courts to issue a writ to the agency staying revocation of the license until the final decision has gone through the entire court appellate process.

In regular criminal court cases, the trier of fact (jury or judge) has to be convinced by the prosecutor of the guilt of the defendant beyond a reasonable doubt. In civil cases, this burden of proof is on the plaintiff to convince the trier of fact by a "preponderance of the evidence." This latter burden is much lighter and means that there just has to be a little more evidence in favor of the plaintiff.

Administrative proceedings are not criminal. The preponderance rule is applied. The burden of proof is on the applicant in a licensing case; it is on the agency in a revocation case.

In these nonjury administrative hearings, matters usually proceed much more informally than in regular court cases. Frequently, persons represent themselves. The normal rules of evidence are relaxed, and hearsay evidence (testimony as to what someone else who is not present said) is admitted.

Don't shy away from Administrative Law in law school. Whether you are with a big-city law firm or independently practicing in a small town, it can be a very rewarding part of your practice.

11
LEARNING FROM THE LAW REVIEWS

Almost every law school publishes something known as a law review, which comes out several times a year. The students with top grades act as an editorial board and, under faculty guidance, put out the publication. If you are asked to write for the law review, do it. The experience is terrific and the prestige may help you get a good job after graduation.

The typical pattern of a law review is to have a few leading articles, usually written by some professors or learned lawyers, followed by student notes on current topics and cases of interest.

Law review articles and notes are thoroughly researched and frequently give a fairly good list of important cases related to the main issues discussed. Generally, there is a citation to every statement made. Read these articles and notes whenever you get a spare moment. They will give you excellent background and peripheral material which will greatly enhance your understanding of the cases presented in your casebook.

The best way to find law-review material which relates to a subject in which you are interested is to look it up in the *Index to Legal Periodicals.* Each year a new volume is published, thus keeping the series current.

At the back of this book I've listed a number of articles covering many subjects which should be of great value to you. I've debated putting it here in the text, rather than in some musty appendix at the end, because it's important that you note the titles and really get the feel of how comprehensive and helpful these articles and others like them can be. But in order to keep up the flow and rhythm, I've succumbed to my judgment as to style versus context. Look at the list so you'll know what's there. It won't mean much to you now, but later, when you're in the middle of some tough subject, you'll really appreciate what help it can be.

Besides law reviews, there are other books which you should become acquainted with over the years. A good book to read for recreation is Martin Mayer's *The Lawyers,* an excellent survey of the entire legal profession written by a journalist. It gives you a great idea of the many facets of law practice; everything's in there from the seedy, little lawyers to the snobbish characters who feel superior because they're lucky enough to have wealthy clients. Although the book was published some years ago, it still has a lot of meat in it.

And by all means, get friendly with the Mr. Tutt stories by Arthur Train. He takes a legal point and wraps an excellent tale around it. It's all common law stuff, so you learn as you read. He wrote primarily in the 1920–30 period.

When I was in law school, I came across a dusty set of books written aroknd 1900—they actually were wrapped up with cord, and the package bore the seal of the county clerk impregnated in red wax. Pasted on the package was a news clipping, musty with age, which told how these particular volumes had greatly aided the criminal element because the author had taken important cases in criminal law and fictionalized them to show how to beat the law. If memory serves me correctly, they were called *The Randolph Mason Stories.* I got the librarian's permission to open the package and found that they were great tales which could give me a good insight into the common law criminal procedure course. The leading character, Randolph Mason, would advise his clients exactly what to do when committing crimes so they could not later be convicted. Each story was cited to an actual case. It was easy for real criminals to follow the fictionalized situations so that, if caught, they would be freed on a legal technicality at their trial. No wonder the poor county board of supervisors thought they had better take these books out of circulation.

Always be on the look-out for this type of material—it makes for relaxing and enjoyable reading and you learn something while you read. And, in this vein, you should read everything and anything that comes your way. After all, law as a profession encompasses all human activity—you never know when something new will be the subject of a case—and the broader your base, the more apt you'll be to come up with an understandable solution to whatever problem presents itself for analysis.

I recently used an article on time travel which appeared in the Mathematical Games section of *Scientific American*. At issue was whether a contractor whose license had expired could still qualify as low bidder on a state construction job if he reactivated his license retroactively. The state's position was that it would be improper to permit him to do so because his status was not equal to that of the other bidders at the time the actual bid was made. The other side argued that the statute permitted retroactive reinstatement for all purposes upon payment of the late annual license fee which had resulted in suspension of the license.

The magazine article which I used pointed out that, if you went back in time and just were an observer, there would be no problem when you returned to the present. But if you went back in time and changed material facts (killed your grandfather, perhaps), you never could reexist in the present because you never would have been born. This paradox has been solved by science fiction writers through the use of the literary device of describing two planes of existence—changing prior facts splits everything thereafter into two parallel worlds, one real and one imaginary or a fantasy.

I successfully argued that retroactive reinstatement of the contractor to give him a license at the time of the bid opening (when he really didn't have one then) was the same kind of paradoxical time travel; acceptance of his theory of the law would put him into the world of fantasy.

12
A QUICK LOOK AT FIRST-YEAR COURSES: CONTRACTS

The big four courses of first-year law school are Contracts, Torts, Crimes, and Property. Generally speaking, Contracts covers the law applicable to individuals who enter into agreements with each other; Torts develops the liability for damages when one individual injures another; and Crimes concerns prosecution of the individual by the government for violation of laws prohibiting certain conduct. Property covers land problems and the laws relating to ownership.

In this and the next three chapters we'll take a look at some aspects of each of these subjects, without attempting a full analysis of any of them, in order to give you some idea of what to expect when you commence your studies.

Your first contact with Contracts will possibly be through some obtuse old English cases which essentially boil down to the proposition that a contract is a *legally enforceable* agreement between two persons. That's the key. If there's an agreement that can't be sued on in a court of law, then you don't have a contract as the law understands it.

Boy meets girl in the local supermarket. Because of their expressed mutual interest in the various brands of anchovies on display, she invites him over for the following Saturday night so together they can discover what makes the water from the whirlpool jets spin in a counterclockwise direction. He agrees to be there at seven-thirty with the proper-colored wine for the occasion.

If he doesn't show, can she sue him for the cost of the new bikini she's purchased, or the spectacular crab-stuffed steak she's prepared?

Anybody can sue anybody. The lawyer asks the question another way. Does she have a cause of action against him? (If she does sue, will a court say there are legal grounds for recovery of damages?) The answer here is no. The agreement to meet on a date is not one which the parties or society intended to be legally enforceable.

Change the facts a little. He's a professional photographer; she's a professional model. He asks her to meet him at the same place so he can take some pictures for a fashion magazine. He's used her before and knows what her customary fee is. It is mutually understood it will be paid. As an aside, both of them probably have visions of using the therapeutic watering facilities after the modeling session as the beginning of a very enjoyable evening. In this case, however, if he doesn't show, she has a valid cause of action against him for her fee. If she doesn't show, he has a valid cause of action against her for his loss of time.

In the first example, the agreement to meet was just a social situation. In the second, there was a business agreement which the law will enforce.

In reality, she may never sue him, or he may never sue her. (Somebody reading this is bound to say they know people in the business, and if anybody in such a situation sued they'd be crazy, because they'd be blackballed and would never get another job in that town.) That's not the point. When you are studying law, you are given factual examples to illustrate principles of law. You learn to take what's presented, isolate it, and apply the rule. Then you start changing facts, adding something new, and testing the rule under different circumstances.

It is extremely important to be aware of this all through law school. Frequently, you'll have some outside knowledge which will make it difficult for you to accept the factual situation presented in the case at hand, or else your own practicality will make you ask, "How could anybody prove that actually occurred?" The best way to handle your problem is to think: *Assuming* these facts are true and that the people really did act that way, what principle or rule of law is applied under those particular circumstances?

Although you may often believe that the law is *applied* in an illogical way, you will gradually realize that there is a certain kind of logic to the way it has developed and the way in which the structure of each branch of law is built up to make the totality of all of it viable and usable in the everyday living experience.

PARTIES

If you look a little closer at the elementary definition of a contract noted above, "a legally enforceableagreement between two persons," perhaps you'll get a clearer idea of what I have in mind.

Focus on the word *persons.* You normally would think it covers anybody, and not go any deeper than that. But the law says, "Wait a minute; there are different kinds of persons: men, married women, single women, senior citizens, children, idiots, the insane, prisoners, slaves, drunks, etc. We're not going to let all these kinds of persons make contracts. Public policy requires that we have special rules for special circumstances."

All these persons can enter into "agreements" if they choose, but those agreements are only legally enforceable if they are contracts. Your Contracts casebook will have a section of cases setting forth the principle that, in order to have a contract, you must have parties capable of contracting.

At common law, married women couldn't enter into contracts; single, adult women and widows could. A wife was considered as one with her husband. He was legally responsible for all the business activity of the marriage. Slaves were considered to be personal property, not legal persons. They could not enter into any contracts. And persons convicted of felonies lost all civil rights.

Drunks, surprisingly, could enter into contracts, possibly because of the underlying community belief that they were responsible for getting into that state, and if they weren't strong enough to hold their liquor they should suffer the consequences. Or perhaps it was because drunkenness was so prevalent that nobody thought of it as a legal disability.

The early common law recognized, however, that idiots did not have the mental capacity to understand enough of what was happening to enter into contracts. Old senile people and insane people did not fare as well. Later on, however, the common law recognized that, if one of these individuals did enter into a contract which was grossly unfair, it could be set aside.

That leaves us with the children. In legalese, they're called "minors." You will find a number of cases in your Contracts book on the rules applicable to minors. You'll probably also pick up some material on minors' contractual obligations in a course called "Persons" or "Domestic Relations."

Basically, if you dealt with a minor, even though you were unaware of the fact of the minority, you did so at your peril. A minor could enter into a contract with an adult, but only the adult was legally bound to perform. At any time during minority (under twenty-one years of age) or for a short time after coming of age, the minor could get his money back by offering to return what he had received in the transaction. If the minor had used it up, the adult would still have to pay.

Timothy Lithe, an energetic, seventeen-year-old businessman, contracts with Robinson Broadbottom, an adult, to buy the peaches on Broadbottom's trees, payment to be made within ten days after the crop is picked. Tim and his crew do the picking, take the peaches to market, get the money. Tim pays off his crew and spends the rest of the money on the pleasures of life. Broadbottom sues for the contract price of the peaches. Tim pleads the defense of minority. Broadbottom loses the case and is left sitting on his name, lucky at least that he still has his trees.

After the 1929 stock market crash, a minor who had started with a small amount of cash became a big operator almost overnight. When the values plunged into the cellar, he was wiped out. He sued his broker, rescinding the contracts he had entered into, and offered to return all the stock certificates that were in his possession. The court decided it was time to modify the common law rule. The minor lost the case; the broker did not have to repay. It was felt that the minor was an astute, knowledgeable investor, and that the basis of the old principle, the protection of minors from being taken advantage of by designing adults, was inappropriate under the circumstances of this particular case.

Thus, a new rule was established: A minor may not disaffirm a stock purchase contract where he or she has essentially the same expertise as a seasoned trader in the market.

This is an example of how the law develops. A basic principle is established. From time to time exceptions are created. Sometimes the principle is totally changed by this erosive process.

If you were in private practice you might, under entirely different circumstances involving a minor's contract, try to generalize this rule, arguing by analogy that the court was really saying: "A minor should not be allowed to use his minority as a weapon against an adult, only as a defensive shield, and then only in those situations where the facts indicated that the minor needed the protection of the law." If the court bought your argument, you would have changed the law in your state. A new building block in the development of Contracts would have been created, to be added to the total structure of the subject.

Let's go back to our original, elementary definition of a contract: a legally enforceable agreement between two persons. We've looked at the "legally enforceable" and "persons" parts. Now we'll zero in on "agreement."

The catchwords and phrases you'll be immersed in are *offer, acceptance, consideration,* and *public policy.* This is one of the early places where you'll be exposed to the "or/ee" syndrome. Lawyers love to tack these syllables onto the ends of words just as the physicians toss out the "otises" and "ituses" when discussing their patients' problems. And so you'll pick up new jargon like offeror, offeree, lienor, lienee, mortgagor, mortgagee, payor, payee, donor, donee, etc.

The "or" ending indicates who the actor or moving party is in the situation; the one who initiates something causing someone else to react. The "ee" ending stands for the party on the other end who gets whatever it is that the "or" party is putting out. Thus, an offeror is the person making the offer; the offeree is the one to whom the offer is made. A purchaser of land gives a mortgage back to the seller for the balance of the purchase price: The purchaser is the mortgagor; the seller is the mortgagee.

One of the things you'll probably have a lot of fun with is give-and-take banter with other law students, bouncing this and other new language around and applying it to everyday things as you try to get used to it and make it a part of your mechanical thinking response.

Remember, though, activity of this sort is a type of "in joke" and, to the lay person, you may sound like a pompous idiot. Some lawyers never realize this and, even after law school, talk as if they have marbles in their mouths. Stuffy, boring, and pedantic, they put every social contact into some legal frame of reference, and cause their listeners to hold on to their wallets for fear of getting billed for the conversation. In my home town there was one lawyer who was so formal that the townspeople believed when he went to bed with someone he referred to himself as the fornicator and his partner as the fornicatee.

OFFER

You will learn that in every contract there is an offeror who makes an offer to an offeree. Before we can go any further, you'll have to know what an offer is. You'll run into a series of cases in your casebook giving various factual examples where courts found an offer either did or did not exist.

A famous pirate says, "I need money. I am going to unbuckle my swash and sell it for two hundred piasters." Is he offering to sell or just making a declaration of intention to do so?

A now-unknown, former famous movie star says, at meeting a group of her fans, "My Oscar is for sale to the first person who comes along and gives me two hundred dollars." Is she making an offer to sell?

The courts would say there is no offer from the pirate but there could be one from the actress. Why? As you plow through the opinions, you'll see a pattern emerging and a principle evolving to the end that an offer must directly or impliedly encompass a binding promise to do something if someone complies with the terms.

Generally, ads in newspapers describing merchandise and giving prices are not considered offers to sell but are held to be in the nature of requests to the reading public to come into the store and make an offer to purchase at the price quoted. This common law rule has been changed by statute in many states.

You'll learn that reward posters have been held to be offers; that there are all kinds of rules for bidding at auctions; that there are numerous other situations where the question of existence of an offer is often arbitrarily determined by custom and usage in a particular area of commerce. Sometimes the conclusions seem strange; but when the rules of interpretation were first set down, the courts felt it necessary to have some certainty which people could rely on in their customary business dealings.

How long does an offer stay open? If you have what's known as an option, you actually have a contract to keep an offer open for a specific period of time. But suppose there is no option and the offeror or the offeree dies. Suppose the offer is revoked before acceptance. Suppose the offeree rejects the offer and then changes his or her mind. These are the kinds of problems you'll run into in law school.

In order to solve the problems you'll be faced with in actual practice, you should start trying to think creatively early in your law school career. Once you are actually out in the field handling matters for real clients, you should be able to apply old rules and adapt existing principles to new situations. The development of the law can be compared to crossing a river that doesn't have a bridge you can walk over. If it's too wide to jump, then look for stepping stones to help you cross.

One of the interesting things which you will observe as you take additional courses and learn new principles relating to different areas of the law is that, frequently, the theories of one course can be carried over into another. Thus, for example, in Torts you learn about the concept of the "reasonable man," and in Contracts you apply that idea to determine whether a reasonable man would really think that certain language or conduct constituted an offer. This taking of ideas from other areas of the law greatly expands the analytical possibilities for problem solution and is why the more varied legal matters you are exposed to, the better lawyer you become.

The law student learns to define, redefine, analyze into

smaller pieces, split proverbial hairs, imagine eyelets on the ballet shoes worn by angels dancing on the heads of pins. And after all that, the student has to apply the principles and rules learned either directly or by analogy to the tiny part distilled out to see if an answer can be found to the problem presented.

After several years of law school and law practice, this intensive approach should become an almost mechanical thought process. While you will look at problems in much the same way after graduation, you won't realize you are doing so and your solutions to new situations will start flowing more readily.

ACCEPTANCE

Another subject which you will be exposed to in your Contracts course, "acceptance," reemphasizes the active analysis necessary to solve a legal problem. Look for different ways to consider whether a legally valid acceptance occurs.

Are the parties talking about the same thing? In a very famous old English case, somebody insures a cargo on a ship, *Ex Peerless, Bombay.* During the journey, a violent storm comes up and destroys the vessel. It then develops that, outside the knowledge of either the insurance agent or the person insuring the cargo, there were two ships names *Peerless* sailing out of Bombay at about the same time. The insurance agent was thinking of one, the customer of the other. The court held there was no valid acceptance, and consequently no contract, because there was no "meeting of the minds."

The offeree has to know of the existence of the offer before it can be accepted. Bleepo sends Curley a letter offering to sell Bleepo's prize bull for fifteen hundred dollars. Curley simultaneously sends Bleepo a letter offering to buy Bleepo's bull for fifteen hundred dollars. Held:

There is no contract. Cross offers do not constitute an acceptance.

You're wondering what kind of crazy ruling is this. The parties have agreed on a price; they're talking about the same bull; and one wants to buy and one wants to sell. How come there's no contract?

Unfortunately, many of the cases in the reports don't contain *all* the facts. When the judges write the opinions, they are primarily interested in giving their legal reasons for their ruling for use in the case at hand. Generally, they are not writing something to be put into a casebook for student use at some later date.

In the Bleepo bull case, several things might have happened to bring the matter to a lawsuit. Before Bleepo got Curley's letter, somebody may have offered him eighteen hundred dollars for the bull, and he sold it to that individual. When the third party found out Curley wanted it, that person offered to sell it to him for two thousand dollars. Curley bought it and was out five hundred dollars. On the other hand, maybe when Bleepo got Curley's letter, he thought that if Curley wanted to pay fifteen hundred dollars without his even offering to sell for that price, why, perhaps, he'd just raise it five hundred dollars. Or maybe Curley received Bleepo's letter late, two or three days after it normally would have arrived, and had already purchased a bull somewhere else. Perhaps Bleepo then sold it to someone else for less than fifteen hundred dollars and thought he had a contract because of Curley's cross offer.

You'll run into a group of cases discussing the time an acceptance is made; i.e., is it when the accepting answer is deposited in the mail box, or when it's actually received by the offeror? Suppose an offer is made by telegram. What rules are applied when the acceptance is by telephone, telegram, letter, or in person?

Suppose the acceptance has to be made in a particular way, but it is received in some other way before the offer is revoked. It's valid, and if all the other requirements exist, a contract results.

CONSIDERATION

Another major aspect of Contracts you'll face is "consideration." Every contract has to have consideration. The only exception at common law were contracts "under seal." That meant a written agreement was drawn up and signed by the parties who also added the impression in wax made by their personal seal.

The easiest way to understand the meaning of consideration is *not* to think of it as money or something of value. Rather, think in terms of a unilateral (one-sided) or a bilateral (two-sided) contract.

In a unilateral contract, only one party is bound to do something. And that obligation arises only if the other party acts first in response to some offer.

Boring says to Fitch, "Mow my lawn and I'll give you ten dollars." This is an offer to enter into a unilateral contract. At this point nobody is bound. Fitch is under no duty to mow; he can do so or not at his pleasure. If Boring revokes his offer before Fitch starts to mow, no contract arises. But if there is no revocation, and within a reasonable time Fitch does mow the lawn, Boring owes him ten dollars. Fitch's act of mowing in response to Boring's agreement to pay creates a unilateral contract; the act is consideration for the promise.

In a bilateral contract, both parties are bound. A promise is given in exchange for a promise.

Boring says to Fitch, "If you agree to mow my lawn Tuesday, I'll give you ten dollars." Fitch says, "I'll be there Tuesday for sure." Here there's a promise given in response to a promise; Boring promises to pay ten dollars if Fitch promises to mow the lawn on Tuesday. Fitch promises to do so. Although his language is not explicit, a reasonable person would imply a promise from what he has said. Boring is bound to pay ten dollars. If Tuesday comes, and Fitch does not appear, there is a breach of contract. Boring can get someone else to do the job. If he has to pay more than ten dollars, Fitch is liable to Boring for the difference.

It's not enough, however, just to do an act or make a promise in order to have valid consideration for a contract. You have to agree to do something that you don't legally have to do, and this doing or not doing must be the reason you give the promise. In a unilateral contract, the act performed in acceptance of the offer must meet the same criterion.

A busload of kids is hijacked and the governor of the state offers a ten-thousand-dollar reward for information leading to the criminal's arrest and conviction. Carl Kopp, a detective in the county where the offense occurred, is assigned to the investigation. He finds the key clue which solves the case. Even though he knows about the reward and works extra hard hoping to collect it, he's not entitled to the money. He's just doing his regular job. He's under a legal duty to catch criminals. The reward is an offer to enter into a unilateral contract. The act which is performed in acceptance of the offer must be one which the acceptor is not legally required to do. There is no consideration.

Walker tells his nephew he is giving him a five-hundred-dollar watch for his birthday. The watch is only worth ten dollars. The nephew has no cause of action against Walker because there was no consideration for the gift.

PUBLIC POLICY

One of the things you have to look out for in consideration problems is whether the giving of the consideration itself is against public policy. Suppose A, a contestant, promises to pay B, a television announcer, a sum of money if B will promise to give A the answer to the Magic Question on next week's show. B promises to do so, and actually gives A the correct answer. A wins, but doesn't pay B. B has no cause of action against A. The consideration is tainted by illegality (the bribe) and fails because it is against public policy to use the law to perpetrate a fraud or enforce the commission of a crime.

Betting is also against public policy. A promises to pay B fifty dollars if the Rams win by ten points next Sunday. B promises to pay A fifty dollars the other way. No enforceable contract. The consideration is illegal. Neither has a cause of action against the other.

This is the first time I've used "A" and "B" to distinguish the people involved. These appellations are helpful when you're trying to solidify your learning. Get used to them. They make it easier to abstractly apply principles to different factual situations.

There are a number of other rules relating to consideration which you'll become familiar with besides those referred to above. After you learn enough examples, you'll be able to sense whether consideration is valid or not. But for now, just be aware that, without it, you can't have a binding contract.

Other aspects of the study of Contracts include the Statute of Frauds, when a contract must be in writing; third-party beneficiary contracts, and whether third persons, not parties to a contract but who stand to benefit from it, have any cause of action if one of the original parties does not perform as promised; what happens if one side fails to perform; when may rights under a contract be transferred or assigned; where are the parties when they agree to cancel the contract and make a new one.

In recent years, most states have adopted what is known as the Uniform Commercial Code. This is a series of laws relating to commercial transactions such as contracts, sales of goods, bank checks, and other "negotiable instruments."

These laws have taken the common law rules which you study in the cases and have put them together in a logical fashion, standardizing former majority and minority positions into one rule and making it easier for business people to deal with each other. As you study contracts and other commercially oriented subjects, you'll be constantly comparing the Uniform Commercial Code to the common law principles.

13

A QUICK LOOK AT FIRST-YEAR COURSES: TORTS

A course in Torts will cover the law applicable to wrongful acts to persons or property, by which others are injured or their property is damaged, and for which the law gives a remedy.

Before you can have a tort, there must be some underlying duty owed to the injured party.

This language is getting a little dense. Let's look at some examples.

A man on shore sees somebody drowning. He can easily toss out a life preserver and save the other person's life, but instead he does nothing. The wife and children of the deceased sue him for wrongful death. No recovery. He was not under any legal duty to help, and although his conduct may have been morally reprehensible, it was not tortious.

But suppose the man on shore was a lifeguard expressly hired to watch the swimmers on that beach. His inaction would probably constitute a breach of a legal duty owed to the man in the water and a cause of action would lie in tort.

Everyone is under an implied legal duty not to injure anyone else. But the duty to give aid to another will arise only if certain specific legal relationships exist between the parties.

There are three broad areas of tort liability which you will be concerned with in your studies: intentional torts, negligent acts, and liability for inherently dangerous activity. All encompass some ramification of this concept that a duty must exist.

Obviously, an intentional act to injure another will be a breach of the duty not to injure owed to everyone. Among intentional torts are physical violence to the person (assault and battery), false imprisonment, invasion of privacy, malicious prosecution, fraud and deceit, libel and slander, trespass, and damage to or taking real or personal property. Generally, anytime some act that harms another person is done intentionally, a tort arises.

As a joke, A pulls a chair away just as B is going to sit down. B falls to the floor and is injured. This is an intentional tort. Even though no harm was intended, the *act* which caused the harm was purposely done. A cause of action will lie against A.

Even if B is not actually hurt, the law may allow nominal damages if the trier of fact (jury, or judge if no jury trial) determines they should be awarded. And where there is an intent to injure, the trier of fact may also award punitive damages as punishment and as a deterrent to future conduct of the same nature.

A collection agency employee knows Mrs. B is a pregnant widow with four children whose sole income is from her job as a secretary in a factory. She has been paying the agency fifteen dollars per month on some outstanding debts. The agency employee keeps calling Mrs. B at home at three A.M. every morning demanding that she pay more and threatening to tell her boss that she is a deadbeat who should be fired. She gets so nervous from all this harassment that she has a miscarriage. This is a case where punitive damages could properly be awarded by the trier of fact.

Note that many of the intentional torts are also crimes. This means that, besides the individual victim who has a civil cause of action against the perpetrator of the tort (referred to as the tort feasor), the State also has a criminal cause of action arising from the same set of facts. Two separate lawsuits could be filed: a privately brought one for money damages, and a publicly brought one which could lead to fine or imprisonment on conviction.

Most of your study of Torts will be spent on the negligence cases. First you'll have to learn all the various elements which go to make up actionable negligence, and then you'll have to know all the possible defenses.

In order to have a cause of action for negligence, there must be a duty of care owed to another; there must be a breach of that duty; the breach must be the proximate cause of some injury or damage; the injury or damage must be reasonably forseeable as a consequence of the breach of the duty.

The special defenses cover contributory negligence, assumption of risk, and last clear chance. This is the type of terminology you'll be using. Let's see what it means.

The duty of care can arise under the general duty not to injure anyone else, or it can arise under some special affirmative duty which is created by the existence of some legal relationship.

Remember the cesspool case we discussed earlier? There, Elizabeth was trying to show that Merriam the landlord had an affirmative duty to her as a tenant to fix the rotted cesspool cover, and that the breach of that duty caused her injuries. The court, however, ruled that the landlord-tenant relationship did not go that far. But the court did point out that some duty would have existed if Merriam knew of the existence of the defect and Booth did not. At the least, he would have been under an affirmative duty to point out the defect to her.

A unknowingly purchases a can of contaminated beans at a grocery store owned by B. C, a guest in A's home, eats the beans and becomes violently ill. The old cases held that C could not recover from A because, as a guest, there was no special duty owed, merely the general duty not to actively harm another. Nor could C recover against B because the only legal relationship which existed was a contractual one of implied warranty of fitness between A and B. When B sold the beans to A, he warranted that they were suitable for the intended purpose. C was said not to be in "privity of contract" with B. In recent years, there has been a trend in many states to give C cause of action against B. If A ate the beans and got sick, A would have a cause of action against B because of the duty which arose from their contractual relationship.

If you want to make a schematic diagram for the bad beans case, you might come up with something like this:

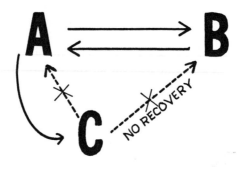

The concept of breach of duty is easy to grasp. Somebody does something that legally they're not supposed to do. It may be based on affirmative interference with another's property or another's right to act in a certain way; it may be a passive refraining from acting toward another in a manner required by some legal relationship; or it may include any conduct in between these two extremes.

A police officer without a search warrant illegally enters a house.

An automobile driver, without looking behind, negligently
   backs into a car which is legally parked on the street.
A chef in a restaurant fails to properly refrigerate the
   cream pies and customers get sick.
A horse rented from a riding stable bucks off the rider.
Because of improper maintenance, a railroad switch sticks
   and one train runs into another.

In each situation above the breach of some duty of care
exists.

At any given time, there are thousands of lawsuits on file
in the courts where negligence is the basis of the action.
Most of them concern recognizable everyday duties of care
which are taken for granted. Occasionally, an astute lawyer
thinks up some new duty which hasn't been recognized
before. The lawyer brings a lawsuit based on it. Frequently,
suits of that nature are unsuccessful, although once in a
while one will stand up to scrutiny. Most of them, however,
are far ahead of their time. Judges as a group are extremely conservative and are reluctant to extend the law
into new areas of applicability based on the theory enunciated in one lawsuit. After a number of suits raising the
issue, and discussion of it in law reviews, this new theory
might be followed. Then other states also use it and the
new theory becomes an established rule.

When new theories like this arise, they usually hit the
newspapers, particularly if they seem outlandish under
present-day knowledge and standards. Some recent examples include the man who sued the store that sold a lady a
very revealing bathing suit. He claimed he was so distracted
watching her that he hit his head going up the ladder to the
high dive board. In another case, a son sued his parents
because he didn't get a good public school education. His
theory was that they acquiesced in his unnecessary absences
from high school and readily gave him false notes to the
attendance office whenever he asked for them.

I once successfully filed a suit on behalf of a client alleging that the defendant, his neighbor, negligently kept a flock of geese which constantly flew over the client's house ". . . and deposited what is commonly referred to as goose droppings on said plaintiff's driveway, which goose droppings when deposited are in a semi-aqueous state and remain so for several minutes." The complaint then went on to allege " . . .that the plaintiff, clad only in a bathrobe, went out to get the Sunday paper, stepped on some newly deposited goose droppings, slipped and tore his bathrobe, injuring his hip and exposing his bare body to the taunts and jeers of sundry and various persons then present in the immediate vicinity of said driveway." This stood up on demurrer, and the court said it had the elements of a valid cause of action.

Like breach of duty, the element of proximate cause is a basic requirement of any tort case. Proximate cause means that the breach of the duty must be connectable through a logical chain of events to the injury suffered by the plaintiff.

Picture an English country fair in the Middle Ages. All the vendors have come early and set up their stalls to display their produce and merchandise to best advantage. One industrious lad has spent the early morning hours making a giant firecracker with a long fuse. By ten o'clock the crowd has arrived. The ale is freely flowing and the firecracker man is glowing. He's there to have fun.

He lights the firecracker and gaily tosses it into the middle of a bunch of vegetables. The excited vegetable man throws it over to the weaver's. The weaver gets rid of it fast and hurls it to the potter. Potter to butcher; butcher to baker; baker to candlestick maker; candlestick maker to draper; draper to picklemonger; picklemonger to—alas, there is no place else to toss it; the fuse has reached the firecracker. It explodes, destroys the stand, and sprays pickles and brine all over the place.

The damaged stall owner sues the original firecracker tosser who pleads the defense that he didn't throw it on the pickle stall; the draper did. The court says that a cause of action arose when the firecracker was first thrown, that the initial toss was the proximate cause in the chain of events which led to the ultimate injury.

When you read this case in law school, the opinion doesn't mention a firecracker; it talks about a "squib." Thousands of law students who never looked up this unknown word have not realized that a squib was really a firecracker, and so they never got the full import of the case. I point this out here so that you'll be reminded to always look up new terms as soon as you come across them.

Closely connected with proximate cause are the doctrines of forseeability and reasonableness.

All through the study of the law, but most particularly in Torts, you'll be running into "the little man who wasn't there." Nobody has ever seen him. He can be male, He can be female. No one knows what clothes he wears. No one knows what he looks like. But every judge and every lawyer will tell you that he should have been at the scene of every negligent tort that ever occurred. Had he been there, like Superman of Krypton, he would have prevented it from happening. He's the mythical "reasonable man" of the law.

The more negligence cases you read, the greater you feel you know him—or perhaps it's the other way around, the less you feel you know him. But he's the character that all actions are tested against. Would a reasonable man act the way this plaintiff or this defendant did under exactly the same set of circumstances? That's the big question in negligence tort cases. Only the trier of fact can answer it. Once the jury finds that the defendant's conduct bears a sufficient causal relationship to the plaintiff's injury, they have to determine whether a reasonable man could have foreseen that the harm would have followed from the conduct.

Some years ago, a Supreme Court justice said that he

couldn't give an exact definition of obscenity, but he knew what it was when he was confronted with it. That's about the status of the reasonable man. Everybody has a sense for who he is and how he thinks, but nobody can describe him with any degree of accuracy. As you study the various cases in Torts, however, your concept of the reasonable man will gradually emerge, and eventually you, too, will have the feel for his amorphous existence.

Besides testing the defendant's conduct, you'll discover that you have to test the plaintiff's as well. Only this time the reasonable man takes the plaintiff's place. The defendant will try to prove that the plaintiff's negligence contributed to the injury. In former days, the finding of the least bit of negligence by the plaintiff would require a defense verdict. This harsh contributory negligence doctrine still exists in many states; however, within the last few years, it is gradually being replaced by the doctrine of comparative negligence. In those jurisdictions following the new rule, the jury is asked to determine the percentage of fault by each party and to apportion the damages between them.

Another defense you'll study is assumption of risk; knowing the risk, the plaintiff nevertheless went ahead and put him or herself in the situation which resulted in the injury. A goes to the baseball game and gets hit on the head by a fly ball. He's assumed a risk inherent in watching the game.

"Last clear chance" is something else you'll run into in tort defenses. It's more or less in between contributory negligence and comparative negligence. If, notwithstanding the plaintiff's contributory negligence, the defendant had the last clear chance to avoid the injury, judgment will be for the plaintiff.

Besides intentional and negligent torts, the third major class of tort cases you'll be exposed to is called "liability without fault," where the defendant is liable for the injury even if he acted with all due care. Here, the liability arises because of the ultrahazardous nature of the activity which the defendant is engaged in; for example, transporting explosives on the highway, experimenting with radioactive materials, dusting crops with poisonous chemicals.

An interesting doctrine you'll also come across in the study of Torts is *res ipsa loquitur*, the proof of negligence through circumstantial evidence. Something happens causing an injury. The victim doesn't know the initial cause. It's the type of thing which is usually the result of negligence. Perhaps the source of knowledge as to its cause is solely within the perspective of the defendant.

A is standing on a sidewalk. A flower pot falls from an apartment window ledge and hits her. In a suit against the tenant who put the pot on the sill, *res ipsa* is used to prove the negligence. The burden is on the defendant to explain what caused the pot to fall.

One reason most students like Torts so much is that it is so easy to relate to. We've all been in auto accidents of one kind or another; we've been exposed to all sorts of injuries to our person and property, fortunately without fatal effects, or we wouldn't be here now considering the study of law as a career.

As you read each case, and after you know and understand the rule clearly, imagine what you would have done if you were the attorney for one side or the other. Is there any way you could have presented the case to achieve victory for your client?

14

A QUICK LOOK AT FIRST-YEAR COURSES: CRIMES

Law school study of criminal law falls into two, or possibly three categories: substantive, procedural, and constitutional.

Substantively, you'll be involved in determining what actually is a crime; procedurally, in the machinations of how it is prosecuted; constitutionally, in the protections set up for the defendant because the state or federal government is the plaintiff in the lawsuit.

As we noted in the last chapter, practically all intentional torts against individuals or property are crimes in most jurisdictions. Interestingly, negligence, too, may be a crime under certain circumstances. Generally, you'll be exposed to the idea that, if conduct is grossly without care (reckless), it may be a crime. Most students are unaware, however, that the bulk of all criminal business, in terms of arrest and action taken, is due to negligent conduct by the defendant. Consider for a moment how many traffic tickets you've gotten and fines you've paid because, unknowingly, you were ignoring a speed limit or a stop sign, or unintentionally violating some other prohibition set forth in your state's Vehicle Code. These and other minor crimes are called misdemeanors; the more serious types of crimes are called felonies.

Classically, at common law, crimes were thought of as *malum in se,* those inherently wrong, and *malum prohibitum,* those prohibited because of some statute. This distinction became important when determining whether it was necessary for the prosecution to prove a specific intent on the part of the defendant to commit the crime. Thus, in a homicide case, the proof of "malice aforethought," or lack of it, could result in a verdict of murder or manslaughter. Much of your first year will be spent grasping concepts like this.

You'll spend many hours studying the idea of attempts to commit crimes and actual commission of crimes attempted. For example: A, clearly intending to kill B, hides along a lonely stretch of road one dark and stormy night, rifle in hand, waiting for what seem like interminable hours. Although no one is anywhere in the area, A mistakes a moving tree branch for B and shoots at it. Assuming that these facts could be proven, has A committed attempted murder? Change the facts just a little: C comes walking along and A shoots and kills him, thinking it is B. Change them again: B comes along alone, A points the rifle, but alters his plan and doesn't shoot. Let's try one more change: A points the rifle, but just as he shoots at B, a deer runs across the line of sight and is hit by the bullet.

The legal rule which ties these cases together (put into the verbose jargon of the law) is that an attempt is itself a crime if there is a present intent to commit some crime coupled with an actual ability to commit that crime, and some overt act is done toward the actual commission of that crime. Generally, the punishment for an attempted crime is less severe than if the crime is actually committed.

One of the reasons for the wordiness is the desire to be as precise as possible so that at least those persons having to apply a rule will do so with consistency. Law is far from an exact science, however, and that is why there frequently are opposite verdicts when two persons are charged with the same crime, and even when the same person is tried twice because of some procedural error in the first trial.

A, suspecting he is being set up for the sale of heroin to

an undercover narcotics agent, passes ten bundles of a mixture of white flour and milk sugar in exchange for the purchase price agreed upon. Here there is an intent to cheat, not an intent to sell a narcotic substance (even though there was an intent to make a buy); and there is no present ability to consummate the transaction. (No contraband passed between the parties.) So the traditional analysis would be that A could not be successfully prosecuted for an attempt to sell heroin. However, he could probably be prosecuted for obtaining money by false pretenses, or larceny by trick and device. Interestingly, because of this legal distinction, many states have passed "turkey laws" making it a narcotics crime to sell imitation narcotics to police agents.

Look for intent-ability questions on law school and bar exams. Frequently, they're subtly disguised in a question such as, "What crime or crimes, if any, has A committed?" In the same type of question, be aware that, if two or more people are engaged in a course of possible criminal conduct, the examiners may want you to discuss the existence of the crimes of solicitation (asking someone to commit a crime), conspiracy (agreeing with someone to commit a crime—conspiracy to commit a misdemeanor is a felony), aiding and abetting (being present and helping in some way but not actually taking part in the crime itself—i.e., driving the criminal to the scene), accessory before or after the fact (being absent, but participating in the crime by ordering it to occur, advising in its commission, instigating it, or hiding the criminal afterwards), or compounding a felony (victim agreeing not to prosecute in exchange for reparation or bribe not to testify).

In the substantive law of Crimes, you'll also be exposed to various crimes and the elements of each. You will find a number of crimes divided into degrees, first degree being the most serious.

The distinction between first- and second-degree murder gives some students trouble. Generally, first-degree murder requires a specific intent to kill the victim, premeditation (plotting in advance), and deliberation (reflecting on the deed in advance). The issue gets sticky when the premeditation and deliberation occur within an extremely short time period after the intent arises. Second-degree murder occurs when intent exists but premeditation or deliberation is lacking. Allied with these concepts is the felony murder rule: If an unintended homicide occurs during the commission of certain "big" felonies such as rape, kidnapping, arson, robbery, burglary, first- or second-degree murder may result, depending on the jurisdiction.

A, a burglar, is apprehended in an unlit store. As he is climbing to the roof trying to escape, an officer shoots at him. The bullet kills A's partner B, the lookout. A can be charged with felony-murder.

The next step down from second-degree murder is voluntary manslaughter. The intent to kill exists, premeditation and deliberation are absent, but mitigating circumstances (generally some reasonable provocation) exist which make for a lesser crime. Under some circumstances, no intent to kill exists, but the defendant has acted so recklessly that he is convicted of involuntary manslaughter.

First-degree Murder: intent, premeditation, and deliberation exist (with malice aforethought).

Second-degree Murder: intent exists; premeditation and/or deliberation absent (no justification).

Voluntary Manslaughter: intent exists, but crime occurs during heat of passion.

Involuntary Manslaughter: extreme recklessness.

There's an old saying that, when the jury in a first-degree murder case comes in with a manslaughter verdict, you can hear the defendant's *man's laughter* permeating the courthouse from silver dome to cellar dungeon. Old courthouse habitués like to tell the story about the friend of a defendant in a famous murder case who bribed a juror to hold out for voluntary manslaughter. After several hours and many ballots, voluntary manslaughter became the final verdict. As the juror was being paid off in the back of a nearby bar, he boasted of his accomplishment, saying, "This was really a tough one. The rest of the jury kept voting for acquittal, but I finally held out long enough to get them to compromise for voluntary manslaughter."

Aside from homicide, you'll also study the elements of a number of crimes such as assault, battery, robbery, mayhem, rape, kidnapping, the various types of larceny (theft, embezzlement, false pretense, trick).

One thing to point out here, which most people are unaware of, is the difference between burglary and robbery. Burglary is the entry of a building with the intent to commit some crime; robbery is theft from the person by force or violence.

At common law, for burglary to occur there had to be a breaking and entering of a dwelling house in the nighttime. Today, in many jurisdictions, a burglary occurs if there is any entry into any building at any time with the intent to commit some crime. For example, people have been convicted of burglary for going into a department store with the intent to use a fraudulent credit card. In some states, statutes make breaking into a locked car to steal something burglary.

There are also certain substantive defenses for crimes which you will become familiar with. You will be surprised when you learn that the term *insanity* is something psychiatrists strongly object to because it is a legal, not a psychiatric, concept. The legal insanity test is based on an old English case; the so-called "M'Naughten Rule" essentially inquires into the defendant's capacity to determine right from wrong.

A defense which is sometimes argued, but not too successfully, is intoxication. If self-induced, the courts will usually say that a person is responsible for all acts committed while under the influence. In recent years, however, probably because of strong arguments against the death penalty, some courts are permitting a defense of diminished capacity (which may or may not result from intoxication) in murder cases.

An interesting defense is that of infancy; the person is too young to form a criminal intent. The common law conclusively presumed children under seven years old incapable of committing any crime, had a rebuttable presumption between seven and fourteen, and considered them adults if over fourteen.

The criminal procedure part of the Crimes course is closely related to guaranteed constitutional protections for the defendant. Criminal procedure is the process of trying and punishing the defendant for the crime.

There are fifty-one separate jurisdictions in the United States, fifty states and the federal government. Each has its own set of criminal laws and each has its own rules of procedure. The lower courts in each state are bound by the decisions of the higher courts in that state and also by the rulings of the United States Supreme Court. If a state wants to, it can give its people greater protection than the United States Constitution requires.

The local federal courts (called district courts) are bound by the rulings of the circuit court for the circuit in which they are located and by the United States Supreme Court. On a federal constitutional question, a local federal court can in a proper case (*habeas corpus,* for example) overrule even the highest court of a state. Many people erroneously believe that the entire Bill of Rights specifically applies to state law. This is not necessarily so. Only that language of those first ten amendments to the Constitution which the United States Supreme Court has declared to be applicable is so.

In this connection, there is an ongoing legal controversy over whether or not the Fourteenth Amendment makes the entire Bill of Rights applicable to state law:

No state shall make or enforce any laws which shall abridge the privileges or immunities of citizens of the United States; nor shall any State deprive any person of life, liberty or property, without due process of law; nor deny to any person within its jurisdiction the equal protection of the Laws.

The Supreme Court has refused to agree with this argument. While many of the justices have indicated a belief to that effect from time to time, they have been extremely cautious in spreading the blanket over all the states, preferring to expand the constitutional protection on a case-by-case basis.

The "Warren Court" expanded criminal defense protection in a number of areas, some of which is now being retrenched by a court made up of different justices. This is compatible with the past history of the Court where the criminal defense protection expands or contracts from time to time. But there is one major contribution to legal analysis engendered by the Warren Court which will continue for many years.

Until the Warren Court, it had always been the rigid rule that, if something were determined to be unconstitutional, it was to be considered so from the beginning of the constitutional enactment on which it was based. Thus, when the Court determined that it was a violation of due process and equal protection to deny an indigent defendant a lawyer at a felony trial, the Court had to rule that all defendants who were in the same category also were denied due process and equal protection. The result in that case was that thousands of "hardened" criminals in all the states had to be retried, or released.

The public outcry was tremendous. And when the Court

started looking at other constitutional protections in procedural situations, such as use of confessions made without knowledge that a lawyer had to be present and provided for if one were requested, the clamor from the citizenry and law enforcement personnel grew louder and louder. But the Court stood fast and retrials upon retrials were ordered throughout the land. Evidence previously thought valid was declared inadmissible and, again, many hardened, confessed criminals were set free.

But gradually, without much awareness by the public even to this day, the Court started to erode the doctrine of retroactive unconstitutionality so that, by the time Chief Justice Warren retired, the rule was established that a decision could be nonretroactive if the Court said so. The result is that we now find decisions being made prospectively. Occasionally, the Court sets up a new interpretation which is not even to be applied in the case before it which resulted in that particular decision.

While this obviates the necessity to open the jail doors to all convicted persons in similar situations, it has another effect which may in the long run be more dangerous to the health of the country.

Prospective decision making is essentially judicial legislation. A simple majority of five judges can now tell the entire United States what the law will be in the future, thus compromising Congress's power to enact statutes which, under the former rule, would have been enacted before being passed upon by the Court. Now, the Court can set down a rule for the future without any statute existing for the court to pass upon, a rule which in effect tells Congress in advance it may not enact a certain statute.

This prospective decision making trait has been picked up by several state supreme courts and a similar situation is starting to exist in their relationships with state legislatures.

Today, in every state, felony crimes are prosecuted either by indictment by a grand jury or an information filed by the prosecutor. In the federal system, the Constitution requires an indictment. Under the indictment system, the prosecutor just presents the government side of the case to the Grand Jury. If they think it shows a crime has been committed, they issue an indictment. This becomes the complaint in the criminal trial. Under the information method, the prosecutor files a complaint directly against the defendant. A public hearing is then held before a magistrate to see if there is probable cause to hold the defendant to answer. Recently, the Supreme Court of the United States ruled that a hearing must now be held in indictment as well as in information cases.

The defendant is given an opportunity to enter a plea before trial. The plea may be Not Guilty, Guilty, Not Guilty by reason of insanity, or Nolo Contendere (no contest). For all practical purposes, the Nolo plea is similar to a plea of guilty; however, it is not an admission of guilt which could be used in a civil case as an indication of liability. On the other hand, a plea of guilty, or a finding of guilty on trial, may be used in a civil case under many circumstances.

All defendants are entitled to a jury trial if they wish one. They are entitled to a lawyer at all stages of the proceedings; if they cannot afford one, the state must provide one at no cost.

After arrest, and during trial, the Court may admit the defendant to bail.

If the verdict is Not Guilty, the defendant is free. If it is Guilty, a probation-and-sentence report is ordered. Based upon this report and other information which may be available to the judge, the defendant is put on probation or sent to jail for the term prescribed by law. The defendant may be paroled prior to expiration of sentence. Violation of parole may result in reincarceration. Upon expiration of sentence time, the individual is freed from all custody.

At the completion of the trial, if found guilty, every convicted person is entitled to appeal. Again, a lawyer is provided free if the defendant cannot afford to pay for the services. Normally, the prosecution may not appeal after a Not Guilty verdict.

Experience has shown that appointed counsel, particularly paid public defenders, do an excellent job at both trial and appellate levels. Many people have a mistaken idea that public defenders are hack lawyers. But frequently, these dedicated public servants do a much better job than the lawyer in private practice who takes the case for a fee. Public defenders are specialists; a private general practice lawyer is not. Public defenders have investigative resources open to them which the private practitioner cannot touch because of the expense to the client. Public defenders argue against the same lawyers from the D.A.'s office on an almost daily basis. This is not to deprecate the work a good, conscientious private practitioner can do for his or her client; rather, it suggests that gross classifications of legal ability based on common misconceptions are frequently unjustified.

As you study Crimes, you will gradually get the deep feeling that our Constitution is a truly wonderful document and that the rights it provides to all persons are simply spectacular. As you approach a career as a lawyer, you'll get a new concept of the right of an individual not to be required to testify against herself or himself, the right of equal protection, the right to be free from unreasonable and warrantless searches and seizures, the right to due process, the right to trial by jury, and all the other rights, some of which have not even been enunciated yet. You'll gradually come to understand that, while it may sometimes seem bad for society to give criminals so many rights, it would be worse if those same rights did not exist to be used when necessary by all of the people. Consider that every right which may be enforced to benefit some terrible criminal is also from then on enforced to protect the average citizen when he or she gets into trouble for perhaps the first time in his or her life.

There's lots to learn, but if you do it systematically, confidently, and calmly, you'll come out okay. As you read the cases, study the prepared outlines, scan the law review articles, browse through the texts, discuss the points with your peers, and listen to the professor's remarks in class, the subjects will become clear, intelligible, and unforgettable.

15
A QUICK LOOK AT FIRST-YEAR COURSES: PROPERTY

Probably the most complicated of first-year courses is Property. The concepts and subject matter are relatively foreign to the experience of most people.

The personal property part is fairly easy because it's familiar. Questions will be raised as to who owns the water in a river as it passes through someone's land: suppose it's wintertime, and the river has frozen to solid ice; or perhaps it's an especially arid summer, and the water has vanished into the ground.

You'll consider the rights of recovery an owner of lost property has, and discuss cases such as the one about the woman who buys an old safe from the Salvation Army and finds a diamond ring that has fallen behind one of the panels.

An area of interest will revolve around something called "fixtures," those sometimes hybrid pieces of property which may take on the real or personal characteristics, depending on the situation. Do the window shades go with the building? How about large fruit trees in big, oaken half-barrels lining the driveway? What about the two-ton statue of Aphrodite's grandmother sitting in the middle of the front lawn?

You're getting in deeper when you get to real property questions. What's the solution when someone purchases a piece of land described in complicated surveyor's language and the survey is wrong? There's one case where the surveyor got turned around 180 degrees and came back on the same line. Suppose a building is built on the wrong lot? Who owns the land from the curb to the middle of the street?

You'll study the various forms of deeds and the effect of technical language used in them. One of the old law school jokes is about the rule in Shelley's case. The rule itself is unimportant until you get into law school. But the story has it that a professor asked an unprepared student to state the "rule in Shelley's case." The quick-witted student, not really knowing the answer, glibly replied, "The rule in Shelley's case is the same as the rule in any other case; the law does not discriminate between persons."

Once you get away from this type of material, you'll get into rather complex problems called "future interests" and "estates." These areas relate to how title to property (who owns it) can be split up between different people. For example, an individual may own the entire piece outright, with no other person having any interest. Or two people may have equal interests.

Then you get into titles held for life, or until a specific event occurs. Suppose someone gave a city some land for a park "so long as no liquor is ever sold thereon." Or perhaps the deed reads, "so long as St. Paul's Church shall stand." In London, St. Paul's Church had been standing for several hundred years. Did the donor mean the gift was forever? What would have happened if it had been bombed to ashes in World War II?

Much of real property law comes from the old English way of holding title. If you owned it outright, you were said to own it in "fee." You'll learn that there was something called "fee tail," which meant that it had to be kept in the family. "Fee tail male," or "fee tail female" meant it went down the line to male or female relatives only.

You'll get involved in ownership of land without any papers or deeds. It's called "adverse possession." Is there such a thing as "squatter's rights?" Suppose you just go onto someone else's property and stay there for years. Can they get you off?

Other areas of study include easements (right to use someone else's land in some limited way as if you were the owner) and specific performance (right to have a court order a transfer of land to be completed).

The best way to be able to handle real property problems is to go to the law library before the semester starts and read as much as you can in as nontechnical language as you can find. Look at some of the law review articles I've listed in the selected list at the back of this book. Some of the works on English legal history by Pollack and Maitland, or Holdsworth, are most helpful. You might even browse through a handbook for real estate brokers at the regular public library to get an elementary, lay person's approach to the subject.

I once heard of some students studying together who had devised a Monopoly-type board game to help them remember how to get through future interests.

Generally, however, if you do not let yourself be awed by the scope of Real Property, and do the initial preparation which I've suggested you do for every course, including looking up all unfamiliar terms in your law dictionary, you shouldn't get into any serious difficulty. Once you can vocalize and visualize what the problems are, the solutions will flow rather rapidly.

16
SOME OBSERVATIONS ON CONSTITUTIONAL LAW

Of all the courses you'll study in law school, Constitutional Law will probably be the most exciting, for the Constitution is the ultimate law of the country. The way it is interpreted can mean the allowance or prohibition of any federal, state, or local governmental activity. Generally speaking, that's what the study of Constitutional Law is all about. Some governmental activity is challenged and the Supreme Court tells us whether it is valid or not. Things which have continued for years without change suddenly are altered because some lawyer has conceived of a new theory which the Court accepts. Most of the time, however, your research will show that the ideas have been around for a long time and attempts to put them across have been orchestrated before other courts for a number of years.

How do new ideas get generated in the first place? Let's look at Article I, section 8, subdivision 1, of the Constitution:

1. The Congress shall have the power to lay and collect taxes, duties, imposts and excises, to pay the debts and provide for the common defense and general welfare of the United States; but all duties, imposts and excises shall be uniform throughout the United States;

The thinking lawyer will read this and perhaps observe that, while Congress is given the "power to lay and collect taxes, duties, imposts and excises," only "duties, imposts and excises shall be uniform throughout the United States." Then this lawyer will think: Four things relating to collecting money are mentioned, but only three require equality. Since the clause specifically omits any admonition about uniformity of taxes, is it possible that this means Congress has the power to levy taxes on property throughout the several states in an unequal manner, i.e., at different rates? How about incomes as well? The Sixteenth Amendment doesn't say anything about equal income taxes, and we know that there are different rates in effect, although everyone in the same class pays the same rate. What effect does the equal protection clause of the Fourteenth Amendment have on this theory?

Let's take another example. The First Amendment provides that "Congress shall make no law *respecting* an establishment of religion. Does "respecting" mean "having respect for," or "in regard to"?

As you go through all your courses you will gradually pick up different ways of looking at words and will realize that sometimes new concepts arise in areas which have been considered solid and unchangeable for years, all because some lawyer saw things from a different angle.

Generally, there will be little stress on constitutional and statutory interpretation outside of your Constitutional Law course, and not too much there either. This is something you'll have to pick up by yourself after you get into private practice. There are numerous rules, often contradictory, but they're all laid out in the legal treatises and encyclopedias you can find in any good law library. They have been developed over the years by the courts and are used to rationalize a position which it is deemed desirable to reach.

Years ago a learned judge wrote an article in which he described the process of appellate judicial thinking. He concluded that the judge writing the opinion first gets a

subconscious bias which permeates his analysis and ener-
gizes his research in a particular direction; then he reaches
his conclusion and goes looking for law to back up his
position, creating new rules if necessary by stretching old
rules almost beyond recognition, but always leaving the old
rules identifiable so that it may be claimed he really used
the old rule and didn't change anything.

This brings us to the doctrine of *stare decisis*. It means
that courts are bound by cases previously decided. The
theory is that the law which rules a community of people
should be certain, specific, and available to all the people of
the community, and that after the law has been announced
by a court in a decision, that decision is the law of the
community until altered either by statute or a new court
decision. In other words, the courts decide cases based on
precedents. Words written by long-dead hands have influence over many years.

It's very frustrating sometimes, particularly if you're an
activist, to see old principles constantly upheld over new
ideas. But, although legal progress is often slow, it does
move on. There is an adage that the essence of law is
change. Almost every newly published appellate court decision moves the law into a different position; some, however, give it a greater shove than others.

It is not only reactionary or conservative judges who
keep the law from changing. Some judges are too lazy to do
the thinking necessary to alter the old precedents. Some
are political cowards and are unwilling to make dynamic
rulings because of a possible adverse reaction at the ballot
box. As a rule, though, most judges honestly are not convinced by the legal arguments advanced in the particular
case before them. Sometimes this is difficult for a lawyer
promoting a new theory to realize because he or she is so
immersed in the case that anyone not taking up the cudgel
on the same side is considered "the enemy."

You must constantly keep a balanced perspective, and no

matter how excited you get about your client's case, always remember that our legal system is based on the principle that the other side has some rights too.

It's amazing how few law students have actually read the United States Constitution from beginning to end. All they have done is studied the cases in their casebooks and read those parts of the Constitution which are referred to in the decisions which have been assigned by their professors.

If you are going to study the law relating to the Constitution, it would seem axiomatic that you first read the Constitution and know its contents in order to intelligently understand how and to what the law is being applied.

When you do your preliminary work for this course before school begins, even before you look up and write the rule at the top of each case, read the Constitution thoroughly. It won't take long. The original Constitution submitted to the states then operating under the Articles of Confederation is only about fifteen pages, and the twenty-six amendments are no more than ten pages. Read it the way you would to prepare your cases for class. First go through the whole thing as fast as possible about five times; then read it from beginning to end intensely about ten times. Even if you use up a whole day, it will be well worthwhile. When you're through, you'll have a pretty good command of the basic source material which you'll be using in this course.

In looking up the cases in a textbook, use the big, fat annotated Constitution of the United States put out by the Congressional Research Service of the Library of Congress. A new edition has come out at ten-year intervals for the past thirty years. It's the best overall work in this field. The book is broken down by direct reference to each clause, and each sentence in it is the rule of a different United States Supreme Court case interpreting the Constitution.

Along with this volume, be sure to read *Miracle at Philadelphia,* by Catherine D. Bowen, published by

Atlantic-Little, Brown. It's an excellent account of the Constitutional Convention of 1787, and will give you great insight into many of the things you'll find in the original Constitution.

One interesting observation you'll probably make after your intensive reading of the Constitution is that the initial part before the amendments is essentially a lawyer's document. By that I mean it is literally packed full of procedural rules that are the wheels which keep the government of the United States moving on a daily basis.

When studying for an exam in Constitutional Law, be sure to have a thorough outline of the Constitution in your head. You'll find it takes only a few seconds to run through the entire thing, and it's an excellent start-off checklist to help you analyze the problems presented.

17
HOW TO ACT IN CLASS

Some of the things I'm going to say in this chapter are rather elementary; unfortunately, however, law students frequently ignore them so it's important to call them to your attention.

First, be as prompt as possible. It's extremely disconcerting to be lecturing to a group and have some clown come staggering in late amidst the snickers and sneers of the rest of the audience. Remember that the professor, regardless of what he or she says, is up there partially because of ego. Just to palliate matters, should you come in late, mouth the words "excuse me" so the professor will notice, sit down as quietly and unobtrusively as possible, and, later on, after the class is over, be sure to walk up and give some short explanation. Try not to be delayed again, at least for a long time.

There are two more things that infuriate many law school professors. One is when a student walks out in the middle of a lecture. If you must do this, be sure, if at all possible, to give the instructor advance notice. Should time be too short to permit an oral explanation, prepare a little note in advance and give it to your instructor before the lecture starts.

The other taboo is to hiss or boo the professor's jokes. This self-image factor is there all the time. Some professors build themselves up by belittling the students; some by always calling on women students to read the sex cases; some have other problems. Once in a while you're lucky to run across a professor who has enough confidence to be really relaxed while putting on a show.

But whether you like it or not, if you want to stay in law school, you've got to let them think that *they* are the fountain of all knowledge and that they have totally intimidated you so that you are mere clay in their hands.

This is a good time to repeat the basic strength motto: *Illegitimus Non Carborundum.* As I was writing this book, I showed my rough notes to law student friends of mine. Many of them expressed the same view and told me to be sure to pass the message on to you. Don't be intimidated! And if you're well prepared, you won't be.

Most law school professors use the Socratic method to teach. They begin class by having a student "give the case" and then they throw things out to try to trap the students into giving inane answers to their questions. Play the game. Try for the right answers at all times, but don't worry if you are wrong. These answers usually don't figure into your grade. They just make the professor feel good because he or she thinks the point is coming across. Generally, the professor only succeeds in confusing unwary students.

And whatever you do, don't worry about how stupid your classmates will think you are. That's what the professor is trying to achieve—your anxiety level being raised by questioning. Laugh with your peers when you get "taken" and you'll be able to laugh louder when they are the victims.

You'll observe during class that most of the students will be constantly scribbling notes, trying to take down everything which is said by both professor and students. Don't follow the crowd. Take down only what the professor says, and be fairly selective about that, too. If he or she is explaining something or giving a summary list, try to get it in full. Later on, you'll want to memorize these notes and cough them up on the exam. If you don't get the full list, see the professor later and make sure that you do.

If something puzzles you, don't wait or pass it off. Ask your question right then, no matter how ridiculous you think it will sound to the rest of the class. Remember, you're in law school to learn something for *yourself*, not to be a paragon of compliance and complacency for the other students. A short, interpretative answer from the professor at the time you need it most can save you hours of hard work later when you are trying to understand the problem. You may have to modify this approach when you have a professor who is an oral grader. See that professor privately.

Be careful how you dress and act in class. Professors tend to be uptight and insecure, and even though they may try to give an impression of relaxed informality, they don't usually appreciate sandals, cut-offs, faddish clothes, three-day beards, sloppy T-shirts, or thermos bottles filled with wine. To cater to this fetish for externals, try coming to class in a plain dress or a vested suit. With that kind of an outfit, your oral grades will probably be higher.

You've got to outsmart the establishment and make your professors believe you fit the pattern which they have set. So, hold back the flippant cracks, laugh at the jokes, let them *think* they have intimidated you, and figure that each day you get through is one less day until graduation and the bar exam.

18
HOW TO STUDY FOR EXAMS

If you've studied your cases for the daily lectures far enough in advance as I've suggested, taken down what the professor has said in class, and done as much outside reading as possible in texts, outlines, and law review articles, you shouldn't have too much trouble taking exams and probably will get fairly good grades.

At this stage, the most important thing is organization. First of all, plan your time so you can start studying for finals at least three weeks before the test date. This is especially important. And you should be completely finished at least two nights before an exam is given. If you wind up cramming the night before an exam, you'll find that you're under great stress while you are taking it and it will be a lot tougher to come up with a good answer. I know that most of you won't believe this advice works; but if you feel you have to look over your notes the night before an exam, at least be sure you've finished studying so that all you do is "look over." Don't leave any learning until the last minute.

The question immediately arises: Should you study alone or with others? After many years of helping friends get through law school and pass the bar exam, I'm convinced that the first study and review should be alone. Do it yourself until you're sure you know the material. Then, go through a short workout with others. There may possibly be a couple of points you've overlooked or have had the wrong impression about. But in the main, you'll find yourself way ahead of your colleagues. Because of your superior knowledge, you'll find yourself teaching and explaining to them. This will greatly reinforce your own learning experience. Additionally, it will send you into the exam with the confidence you need to do your best in the most relaxed manner.

After a joint discussion session, leave yourself enough time to do your own final review. You may find that you have inadvertently picked up a number of wrong approaches to the exam from your colleagues.

I don't want to leave you with the impression that you should be a "loner," however. One of the most valuable aspects of law school is the constant, informal give and take among students where hairs are split and a growing knowledge of the law is applied to outlandish examples.

As to the actual studying itself, it is most helpful to continue the overview approach which I have suggested for daily class case work. First, intensely review the total course in outline fashion. Start by going over the table of contents of the casebook. You should have memorized the major divisions long before now. If not, do so immediately. Then, learn the important subdivisions so that you really have the whole course in mind.

As you do this, certain minor subdivisions will come to mind. Jot them down. For example, you'll frequently find that the general rule for some proposition is divided into a majority and a minority view. Then, perhaps, each of these views is dependent upon what conclusion the trier of fact has reached in a given situation. You should be able to set these variations up into something resembling a geneology table format. The kind of material which exam question designers like to play around with lends itself readily to this kind of an approach. Professors especially enjoy having students regurgitate lists that they heard in class.

Most students don't realize that the purpose of a law school exam question, besides the obvious one of testing your knowledge, is its use as a vehicle by which the professor hopes to guide you into the specific area which he or she wants you to discuss.

To give you a more concrete example of what I'm talking about, there's a doctrine in Contracts called the "Statute of Frauds." It really has little or nothing to do with fraud. What it means is that, unless certain types of contracts are in writing, they will not be enforced by the courts. For example, a contract for the sale of real property must be in writing. Like all major legal doctrines, there are exceptions to the rule. It is the study of these doctrines or rules and exceptions which comprises most of the study of law.

On an exam, if the question says the contract between the parties is in writing, it's generally axiomatic that the professor doesn't want a long discussion on the Statute of Frauds. In most instances, it's enough to note that it's not applicable.

As I write this, I can imagine a future generation of clever professors who will design questions where the contract is in writing and yet the discussion of the Statute of Frauds will be the answer they are looking for.

At the start of any particular course, you won't have too much of a feel for what it's all about. Later on, as your knowledge gains in depth, various parts of the course will fall into logical sequence. It will be extremely helpful when taking exams if you have developed your own category for such groupings. A good way to do this is to make up your own hypothetical case that covers all the elements in the particular segment of the course.

Let's look at the area known as "quasi-contracts," usually part of a course called "Remedies" or "Restitution." For the first several weeks, the incantations sound something like this: "quasi-contracts," "unjust enrichment," "reasonable value of the benefit received," "contract implied in fact," "contract implied in law."

Many students have a murderous time trying to figure

out what the devil is going on. The intimidation dragon is heavily at work trying, as usual, to scare the hell into (not out of) you. Be undaunted, intrepid, and above all relaxed. The overview will help you triumph once again.

Start with Harvey Brown of Middlebore, Anystate, U.S.A. He lives in a tract house across the river in the Blissville area. Every house is exactly the same for miles in each direction. The reason they make each alike is that there's a big conspiracy between the lawyers and the contractors. According to the law of averages, at least once every couple of months somebody is going to come home drunk and walk into the wrong house. That will lead to more divorces, which will lead to more marriages or cohabitations, which will lead to more houses being constructed to take care of more waterbeds being purchased.

One day, Harvey is at the Middlebore Service Club weekly luncheon sitting next to Joe the roofer.

"Joe, old Service Club buddy, how much will you charge me to roof that little place of mine over on Wishing Well Street in the Blissville area?"

"For you, Harv," after thinking a minute and a quick calculation on the tablecloth, "twenty-four hundred dollars."

"That sounds pretty good, Joe. When can your guys get over to do the job?"

"How's next Thursday? Okay?"

"Okay."

This is an actual contract, even though not in writing. It is called a contract implied in fact. Harvey has legally contracted to pay Joe the twenty-four hundred dollars when he's finished the job. They polish off the mashed potatoes and gravy, listen to the guest speaker, and then take off to their offices.

Next Thursday arrives. Joe's men are going over to Harvey's on the roofing truck. By mistake, they miss Harvey's house and hit one just like it on the next street. They put the ladder up against the wrong house, Machiavelli's. Mrs. Machiavelli, hanging out the wash, watches what's going on and thinks, "If I keep quiet, we'll get a free roof job."

Though Joe's people made a mistake, it would be unconscionable to allow Mrs. Machiavelli to profit by the error which she knew of but did nothing to prevent. After all, she's received the benefit of the roof job. The law will not permit her to be *unjustly enriched.* It will imply a *contract in law* to rectify the situation. That means, although the parties (Joe and Mrs. Machiavelli) did not actually have a contract, the law will treat them as if they did.

"Quasi-contract" means "like a contract" and is the remedy which is utilized to put people whole again (where they would have been if nothing had happened), even if there is no actual contract, when one individual is unjustly enriched at the expense of another.

If Joe's men had put up the roof on Harvey's house in accordance with the terms of the original contract and Harvey had not paid, Joe could have sued Harvey for the contract price, twenty-four hundred dollars. But what is the measure of damages (how much can Joe get) in the quasi-contract suit if he has to take Mrs. Machiavelli to court?

The law says it is the *reasonable value of the benefit received.* Here, the roof job may be worth more or less than twenty-four hundred dollars. Joe may have given Harvey a special price. That amount is only some evidence of what a reasonable value might be.

At a trial, Joe himself would testify and would also bring in expert witnesses from the roofing business to state their opinions as to reasonable value. The amount determined by the trier of fact (the jury, or if there is no jury, the judge) would be the amount of the recovery (what Joe gets if he wins).

Suppose if, instead of being home hanging clothes out on the line, Mrs. Machiavelli was away on vacation. Since she did not compound the error because she did not have knowledge of it, she would not have been *unjustly* enriched. She would get a free roof job whether she needed one or not.

The segment of the Remedies course, "quasi-contract" is now all neatly packaged for your subsequent use in the "Joe-the-roofer case," and it's easy to resurrect the principle: "Quasi-contract is the remedy for unjust enrichment. Damages awarded are for the reasonable value of the benefit received."

Without realizing it, you'll gradually find that you are starting to talk like a lawyer. And once you get an area of law like this categorized so you can use it when an analogous situation arises, you'll start thinking like a lawyer too.

I had a great experience with quasi-contracts in my first year of law practice which I'd like to share with you. To help with the rent and also to get known around town as a lawyer, I had been teaching a law-for-lay persons course at the local adult evening school. One of my students dropped in with a case. He had worked about ten years for the biggest bank in the community and was chagrined because he did not receive a hoped-for promotion.

As part of his duties, he had been the bank notary public. The company had paid for his seal, application fee, and official bond premium. It required him to charge notary fees to the small depositors and noncustomers of the bank, but made him do the work free for the bank itself and its big customers. All fees received were placed in a special account in his name; at the end of each month, the balance was zeroed out and the amount on hand was transferred to the company employees' recreational welfare fund.

Huffed at his failure to achieve his promotion, he had quit his job and now wanted to sue the bank for the notary fees.

Notaries are appointed by the governor in most states and are considered to be minor public officials. The law in most states is that the fees an official receives in the performance of his duties are sacrosanct; they belong to the official, and it is improper to refuse to pay them or take them from him. I had mentioned this in class in an offhand way one night, not realizing the special value it would have for this student.

On his behalf, I wrote a letter to the branch manager of the bank, saying something like, "When Joe Blow left your employ yesterday, you inadvertently forgot to pay him for the notary fees which he had collected in his official capacity, and which we have computed to be eleven hundred dollars. Undoubtedly, you will wish to correct this oversight promptly. You may do so by sending your check to him, care of the undersigned. If we do not hear from you within ten days, appropriate legal action will be instituted to collect this sum."

(Be extremely careful about what you say when you write a letter to someone requesting payment of a debt to a client. Never imply that criminal action will be taken if payment is not forthcoming. This is a particularly easy trap to fall into if someone has given your client a bad check, for example. The *threat* of going to the D.A. to collect by prosecution because of forgery or insufficient funds is extortion, a felony. Occasionally, overzealous young lawyers write dunning letters that go over this line, and once in a while they get disciplined by their state supreme court; sometimes they even get prosecuted by the D.A.)

The bank manager called my office about four times the next morning (that was back in the days of quick mail delivery) while I was in court. Although we had met at a few local functions, he'd never been too friendly before. But now, he actually came to my office. He was all frozen smiles and oil; even called me mister when he shook my hand.

Getting right down to business, he told me how I was new in town and what a great future I had ahead of me; too bad I was jeopardizing it by representing somebody like his former employee. After all, trying to get the bank's money like this was tantamount to trying to steal it. The bank had paid all the expenses; what did this ex-employee mean by making such an outlandish claim? In all the years he had been a bank branch manager, he had never heard of such a thing.

By this time, his harangue was getting pretty thick, so I shoved one of the Supreme Court Reports across the desk at him and asked him if he had ever heard of the case on page 198. I then leaned over, picked up the book and read him something like this from the decision I was referring to: "The notary public is the long arm of the Governor in the provinces. It is an offense against the sovereign to refuse to pay or to take from that official his legally authorized fees. Under such circumstances, there is an unjust enrichment for which the notary public may bring an action in quasi-contract against the wrongdoer."

The bank manager quickly changed the subject back to what a great future there was for me; he told me how much business the bank could send me and said they'd be doing a great service for the customers by the referrals, because I evidently was a pretty smart lawyer. Then he maneuvered into the suggestion that it would be the best thing for everyone concerned if he recommended to his committee that they settle this case for one hundred dollars, not because of the bank's liability, of course, but just for the nuisance value involved in the claim.

Although I was seething at this implied bribe attempt, I tried not to show it, and shook his hand as we got up toward the door. Then I said, "That will be great. You make that recommendation to your committee. But tell them I never agreed to it and that it's solely your idea. And while you're telling them that, also tell them that if I don't have a check for the full amount of eleven hundred dollars by noon tomorrow, I'll file suit against the bank for every document he ever notarized for them free within the period of the statute of limitations, and perhaps I'll even file a class action against the bank on behalf of all the other notaries who work for the bank and its branches for the money owed to them."

The bank manager left quickly, the icy smile and oily manners dissolving into his more usual "you bastard" look.

That afternoon, the senior partner of the leading law firm in town called to see what he could do to ameliorate the matter. I told him what happened and cited the case on page 198 of the Supreme Court Report. He said he'd study it and get back to me.

At eleven-thirty the next morning a bank messenger appeared at my office with a check for eleven hundred dollars, payable to me and my client, and a release form for my client to sign agreeing that any claim he had against the bank had been settled.

Some years later, I learned that this particular banking chain had issued an order to all branches that same afternoon which discontinued the use of any notaries who worked for the bank, even for the bank's own documents.

19
HOW TO ANSWER EXAM QUESTIONS

A good answer to any essay exam question will usually include identification of the basic issues or doctrines in the question, a statement of the relevant rules and exceptions, the application of these rules to the facts presented, and a conclusion which logically follows.

Law school questions will generally be confined to the scope of the course. On the bar exam, however, if it contains questions, the examiners will frequently mix more than one subject. In law school the emphasis is more on course content. On the bar, this is vital; but the examiners are also greatly interested in whether you can *think* like a lawyer.

There is a growing tendency to have fewer essays and more computer-correctable true-false and multiple-choice questions on bar exams these days. The principles of analysis remain the same, however. The examiners are still trying to determine whether you should be released to the world and allowed to handle individuals' problems within the framework of the legal system.

For three years, you have been accumulating this special knowledge. How can you make what you have learned work for the best protection of your client?

A good lawyer looks at every problem from all possible perspectives. Remember, every legal problem has adversary connotations. This is easy to see when you're in the middle of a lawsuit, but it's also true, for example, when you're drafting a statute or giving advice on what course of action should be followed in a preventative law situation.

So, when you take any law exam, keep in mind that you are in training to be a lawyer. When I studied for the bar, I took a quiz course given by three people. One taught substantive law—contracts, torts, corporations, etc. A second taught adjective law—practice, procedure, evidence. The third taught how to pass the bar exam.

To this day, I can see that last man, a natural comedian, standing up on a stage smoking a long cigar. He said, "They throw an old lady in your office; she's got three kids—one has polio, another has pneumonia, and the third just flunked her rabbit test; it's snowing outside; the mortgage is due. . . ." Then he threw the cigar on the floor, jumped on it, and yelled, "The answer is no!" His message was clear. On the bar, don't get sucked into a vortex of sympathy so you spin around so rapidly you can't solve the problem presented. This doesn't mean that the answer couldn't be yes. It's just a caution to beware writing like a liberal social worker instead of a lawyer.

The "no" approach is a particularly good technique to use in handling tort and criminal law questions. Remember, you should be able to take either side of any case and give your client the best possible representation within the framework of the law.

Earlier, I mentioned the use of commercially prepared study outlines which you would be wise to obtain. Most of these have detailed methods of problem analysis which have proved effective throughout the years. They will be of immense help on law school exams and, for the bar, they're a must.

Here's a sample bar exam question so you can see how this "no" method works. This particular question has both tort and wills aspects to it.

Mrs. Jones, a woman of exemplary character, appears in your office in a common law jurisdiction and states that her husband has just died and his will is about to be probated. In it, he has called her a common prostitute and has left her only a dollar. Discuss her rights and remedies.

A good answer might run something like this:

The common law of torts is divided into three general areas: intentional or malicious torts, negligent torts, and liability without fault due to the extrahazardous nature of the activity.

Here, in writing, in his will, a husband has accused his wife, a woman of exemplary character, of being a common prostitute. This is defamation of character, a malicious tort. Since it is in writing, it is a libel; were it oral, it would be slander.

No action will lie at common law, however, for two reasons: (1) A husband could not commit any tort against his wife. (2) All tort actions died with the death of the perpetrator of the tort, the tort feasor.

No action will lie against the lawyer who drew the will because any information he received from his client, the husband, was subject to the lawyer-client privilege. This privilege extends to the lawyer's secretary who typed the will.

No action will lie against the executor who filed the will for probate as his act, too, is privileged because he is under a legal duty to make such a filing.

No action will lie against the court or any of its officials because of the privilege afforded to judicial actions.

No action will lie against the estate of the husband because, as previously stated, the tort remedy, if any existed, died with the death of the tort feasor.

[So you see, as of this point, the "no" approach has enabled us to give a broad discussion of the applicable law of torts, setting forth principles and exceptions. To wrap up the question, let's look at the wills part for a moment.]

While there can be no recovery under the law of torts, there are several areas under the law of wills which may afford the wife relief.

Under the majority rule, where a husband is so mistaken as to his wife's true nature that he erroneously considers her a prostitute when she is of exemplary character, such a statement in a will is conclusive evidence that the husband did not have testamentary capacity to make the will himself. His mistaken belief went right to the heart of the issue. His widow should be successful in moving to set aside the will and keep it from being admitted to probate. Under such circumstances, the husband would be held to have died intestate. The widow could apply for appointment as administratrix of the estate. She also gets dower rights.

During pendency of the action, the widow would also be entitled to a widow's allowance.

[If you take the bar in a community property state, throw in a possible extra-credit line or two to the effect that in a community property state the husband could only will away his half of the community property.]

Notice, in particular, that we didn't give any case citation of any kind. The bar examiners don't expect you to be a walking research library. And if you give a wrong citation, they may very well mark you down.

20
HOW TO PUT A BRIEF TOGETHER

One of these days, you're going to have to write a brief. What is it? A brief is a formal, written legal argument made to a court for the purpose of convincing the judge or judges hearing the case that they should rule in your favor. It should discuss each issue under contention, set forth the law applicable to the facts at hand, and point out any flaws in your opponent's position.

In law school, you practice writing briefs in an appellate writing course, if your school gives one, or in Moot Court. Moot Court is a make-believe appellate court. Generally, a hypothetical statement of facts containing several novel legal issues is presented to the Moot Court participants and, working from that, they have to prepare and submit briefs and then argue the case before a simulated judicial tribunal. (In actual practice, you get a reporter's transcript of the trial and have to dig out the facts yourself.)

Moot Court is a good experience and gets you involved in legal research fairly rapidly. Generally, you're given a reasonably long period of time, a month or more, to do your preparation. Start as soon as possible. It takes a lot of effort and, if you procrastinate, you'll do a poor job.

Most lawyers in private practice get very little chance to go into the appellate courts, and consequently are terrified at the thought of writing a brief. Do everything you can in law school to get as much brief-writing experience as you can. It pays off in a number of ways.

Most important, it expands your law-finding ability. As you do your research and think about various possible arguments you may wish to use, you begin to see that there are numerous ways to approach a particular problem. You suddenly discover that the indices to legal literature are only as helpful as the acumen of the persons who prepared them. Sometimes you look up a topic in an index and it refers you to some other word or phrase. Then, when you look at the second place, you are referred back to the first. Other times, you think something is very elementary, but you just can't find anything listed on the subject. After a short time, however, familiarity with the indices pays off in rapid progress in research. The more experience you have, the more you develop new ideas on where to look. Analogous legal doctrines suggest themselves and, frequently, persuasive new arguments arise.

Besides expanding your law-finding ability, brief-writing knowledge is extremely valuable for daily law practice. Most obviously, it helps you look up the law quickly and get right to your client's problem and solution. But where it really pays off is when you file a motion in a court case and have to give the judge a memorandum of law to sustain your position. This is customarily referred to in lawyers' jargon as "P's and A's" (Points and Authorities).

When I first went into private practice, almost every lawyer had a sign on his wall with a picture of Abraham Lincoln and the words: "A lawyer's time and advice are his stock in trade." If you can research and write a memorandum of law fast and competently, you'll be saving time and giving good advice.

With these preliminary remarks, let's look more directly at how to write a brief.

The physical style of brief writing has become fairly formalized over the years. Practically all appellate courts have detailed rules as to size of pages, type specifications, arrangements of contents, etc. Check the rules for the jurisdiction you're in to make sure the clerk will accept your papers when you are ready to file them. Incidentally, be very careful of time deadlines or you may find your appeal is dismissed.

Generally, insofar as format goes, the brief starts out with a title page which gives the name of the court; the name of the case (referred to as the "caption"); the title (e.g., "Apellant's Reply Brief"); the name of the court where the action arose; and the names, addresses, and telephone numbers of the lawyers who are filing the brief.

Where the courts require printed briefs, and most do, there are also specific rules as to what color the cover of each of the parties' briefs must be. This is to help the judges so they immediately know which side of the case they are reading about.

After the title page comes the table of contents (sometimes referred to as "Subject Index"). As in any book, it's usually an index to the material by section headings. I always copy the full section headings in the table of contents.

If there is an intermediate appellate court opinion, that comes next, depending on the jurisdiction you're in.

Then comes a page stating the major issues to be covered in the brief. These are referred to as "Questions Presented." All briefs have one; some may contain more. In writing a question, most brief writers try to get everything into one sentence. Sometimes this gets ridiculously long. If so, I prefer to split one question into two for clarity. My basic thought in writing the Questions Presented is to try and get something special in it which will make the court want to read what I have to say. I consider a brief a selling document. Each title, each word, is carefully selected for its sales effect, to try to get the court to buy my side of the case.

Here's an example of the Questions Presented section

taken from a brief filed in the United States Supreme Court in *Richardson* v. *Ramirez* (1974) 418 U.S. 24, 94 S. Ct. 2655, 41 L. Ed. 2d 551.

QUESTIONS PRESENTED

Can a state constitutionally disenfranchise convicted felons who are otherwise qualified to vote?

a. Does the denial of voting rights for "participation in rebellion, or other crime" language of the United States Constitution, Amendment XIV, Section 2, override the "equal protection" clause of Amendment XIV, Section 1, insofar as a state's right to disenfranchise convicted felons is concerned?

b. May California deny the privileges of an elector to a person convicted of an infamous crime, embezzlement or misappropriation of public money, or exclude from suffrage persons convicted of bribery, perjury, forgery, malfeasance in office, or other high crimes?

The attention getter in these questions is the proposition that the equal protection clause of the first section of the Fourteenth Amendment is actually restricted by language in the second section of the same amendment.

Next in the brief is a section giving the exact constitutional and statutory language which will be referred to later on in the argument part of the brief. If this is unusually lengthy, I think it is more beneficial to include quotations only from the vital sections of the law in this part and the rest in the Appendix. It depends on the rules of court in a particular jurisdiction as to whether this is possible.

After the recitation of the applicable constitutional and statutory law comes what is called "Statement of the Case." Statement of the Case is a summary of the *procedural* history of the case: what happened in the court down below to get the case up to the court where it now is. Some lawyers will mix up *facts* in the Statement of the Case. This irks judges. They have to know how the case arose so that they will know which rules of law to apply to the facts of the case.

The Statement of the Case is prepared from the clerk's transcript ("C.T.") of the record (the copy of the papers on file in the trial court). Each sentence is carefully referenced to show the page where it may be found.

A typical Statement of the Case in a civil matter might look something like this:

Appellant brought an action for breach of contract against respondent in the Superior Court of Marlynn County. (C.T. 1) On July 8, 1979 the trial court sustained respondent's demurrer without leave to amend. (C.T. 34) Judgment for respondent entered September 10, 1979. (C.T. 38) Appellant appeals from the Order Sustaining Demurrer Without Leave To Amend. (C.T. 42)

In a criminal case, you might find something very similar; however, because of the nature of the proceedings, the entries in the record will be different.

On April 1, 1977 appellant was charged by indictment by the Grand Jury of Marlynn County with one count of Grand Theft Auto, violation of Penal Code section 193, subdivision (a). (C.T. 1) A Not Guilty plea was entered. (C.T. 4) After jury trial, he was found guilty on December 3, 1977. (C.T. 96) Motion for new trial denied January 6, 1978. (C.T. 98) Probation for five years granted January 6, 1978, on condition that appellant spend the first six months in the county jail. (C.T. 101) On September 5, 1978, after hearing at which appellant was represented by counsel, probation was revoked and appellant was sentenced to the State Prison for the term prescribed by law. (C.T. 105) Appellant appeals from the Order Revoking Probation. (C.T. 107)

It is extremely important when writing the next section of the brief, the "Statement of Facts," that you be very accurate and limit your description to only those facts set forth in the record on appeal. The information in the Statement of Facts comes from the reporter's transcript of the trial ("R.T."). If there is a preliminary hearing transcript, make up reference letters such as "P.T." and, the first time you use them, explain the meaning in a footnote. As much as possible, try to use the exact language of the record. If you summarize or paraphrase, be as close to the original text as grammar will allow.

Remember that you are trying to give the reviewing court a quick picture of a trial that may have actually taken two or three weeks. If a number of witnesses testify to the same thing, you can capsulize their testimony by using one entry with numerous page citations.

Here's an example taken from a brief in a long murder trial. It is only part of a Statement of Facts which, by necessity, went into more detail on other issues. This part sets the stage of the actual homicide.

On April 17, 1974, Mary Torrent gave a surprise birthday party for Andy Goran. (R.T. 16, 72, 148, 327, 1108) Twenty-three guests were invited in addition to Andy. (R.T. 16 [plus about ten more page citations])

During the evening, appellant, an uninvited person, showed up. [Again, about twenty page citations.] He was drunk when he arrived. [Citations.] He kept drinking heavily. [Citations.]

About 1:30 A.M., because of his drunken condition, Andy asked him to leave. [Citations.] There was a fist fight between them. [Citations.] Appellant left. [Citations.]

A half hour later appellant appeared at the front door with a long knife. [Citations.] He said, "If you come past this door, you bastard, I'll stick this knife in you." [Citations.]

(From here on, I'll not indicate that page citations follow each sentence. Just don't forget them when you work on your Moot Court or actual court brief.)

Andy said nothing and started for the door. Pete Jones and Willie Smith tried to hold him back. Andy brushed them aside and went outside. Everybody followed and made a ring around them. Andy was unarmed.

Appellant said, "I told you I'd stick this knife in you." Andy said, "Go ahead." Appellant lifted the knife. Four of the onlookers rushed to stop him. Appellant stuck the knife into Andy's chest very deeply. The other people pulled him away. Andy fell to the ground.

An ambulance was called. Andy was dead when it arrived.

The police came. They took statements from everybody. Appellant was given his Miranda warning. He said he wanted a lawyer, so there was no further interrogation. He was taken to the county jail.

Try for a reasonably short Statement of Facts. Be sure, however, that you put in enough to support the legal arguments which follow in the brief. Give the court sufficient facts to permit it to apply the legal issues and rules which are involved.

In this particular example, taken from a brief for the prosecution, there is a subtle technique used which is worth mentioning. Note that nowhere is the appellant's name mentioned. Yet, wherever possible, the names of the other witnesses are given. The victim is referred to only once by his full name. After that, he's called "Andy."

Everything has been carefully written to portray appellant as a nameless, faceless, nondescript individual. The victim has been personified as much as possible. This approach is frequently used by prosecution brief writers in order to obtain some psychological edge when the reviewing court reads the summary of the cold record.

A good defense briefer might try something similar. Here's how it might come out. (Again, I'm omitting page citations. Remember, they *must* be given after each sentence.)

On the afternoon of April 17, 1974, Peter Loring, appellant, was working at the checkout counter of the Lucky Boy Market on Wilson Avenue in Corning. Mary Torrent, whom he had known all through high school, was purchasing a whole lot of groceries.

She said she was putting on a surprise birthday party for Andy Goran, the man who was killed.

Peter knew him since they were little kids. They had been good friends, but had drifted apart when Goran started using LSD in his junior year at Corning High. Goran had become a Hell's-Angel-biker type. He was always high on something. Peter took a drink once in a while, but he had seen what dope could do to a guy—he had seen how it wrecked the lives of several of his former classmates. And when he served his tour in Vietnam, he saw a number of guys screw up because of drugs.

Peter and Mary talked for a minute or two—you know how it is at a checkout counter. She left with her groceries. Peter did not see her again until late that night.

After the store closed at 10:00 P.M., Peter and Frank Balba, one of the other checkers, stopped for a beer at the Old Mill Bar. They had two or three bottles apiece and shot some pool. Chuck Turner came in all excited. He had just seen Peter's best friend, Milo Pepper, killed in a fiery car accident over on Murphy's road near the bridge. Tears came to Peter's eyes. He started drinking straight bourbons. After about an hour or so, Peter was pretty drunk. The bartender eighty-sixed him.

The next thing Peter remembered, he was standing at the table in Mary's living room. Goran was making fun of him because he was crying. When Goran said, "I never liked that Milo Pepper bastard, anyway," Peter felt he wanted to kill him. He started throwing punches at Goran; he really wanted to kill him. Goran knocked him to the floor.

Peter left. All he could think of was that he wanted to kill Goran because of what he had said about poor Milo Pepper. He remembered getting a knife and stabbing Goran, he was so angry. The details are very hazy. He remembered the cop telling him he could get a lawyer, that's all.

I think you can get the picture. There are two sides to every case and, given the same transcript of the evidence, there are generally at least two ways to tell the story. However, you must use the language from the record as exactly as possible. But use it to establish the facts in the best way for your side.

Remember, on appeal the reviewing court is looking for any substantial evidence in the record which would uphold the verdict rendered by the trier of fact.

In choosing the facts, don't leave out uncontroverted facts which are against you with the hope that the court won't pick them up. And don't select only favorable matters so that the real state of the record becomes distorted. Present the facts truthfully and carefully in the best light possible. If you're stuck with a bad fact, mention it if it's important and continue on.

Courts greatly resent attorneys for one side or the other trying to give them a distorted picture of the record. Remember the old legal adage: If the facts are with you, argue the facts; if the facts are against you, argue the law; if the facts and the law are against you, bang on the table, yell like hell, and discuss the sociological implications of the situation!

After the Statement of Facts comes the "Argument." This is a discussion of all the issues of law in the case. The idea is to apply the law to the facts in a persuasive way so that the reviewing court will hand down a decision in your favor.

Customarily, the points raised are broken down into separate sections. Each section is set off by a number, more or less in outline form. Frequently, there are also subsections. Each section and subsection is given a title. I always put my titles verbatim into the table of contents. This gives anyone who picks up the brief a good idea of what my arguments are and helps set the right stage for their reading.

Make your titles as positive as possible. This helps "sell" the case. Keep this selling idea in front of you all the time you are preparing the brief. Think of the salesperson in a dress shop. She can show a customer thirty different dresses, but unless the customer makes a purchase, there is no profit in the cash register.

The Argument is followed by the "Conclusion." This should be a short summary of all the major points developed in the brief. Considering the Introduction, the Argument, and the Conclusion, remember the old teacher's advice to neophytes just starting with their first class: "Tell them what you are going to tell them. Then, tell them. Then, tell them what you told them."

If you need an Appendix for long statutes or other material (like copies of pertinent legislative committee reports, for example), put it after the Conclusion. Each item should be separately numbered or lettered as an exhibit to the brief, and should be so noted in the appropriate place in the main text.

21
HOW TO WRITE THE ARGUMENT

The Argument has to raise legal issues which, from the appellant's point of view, will cause the appellate court to reverse the judgment of the trial court and, from the respondent's point of view, will cause the court to sustain the judgment.

In order to find these issues, you have to go through the record looking for possible error. In most jurisdictions, the error should have been pointed out to the trial court or else it cannot be raised on appeal. Because of constitutional questions relating to due process, equal protection, and right to counsel, however, courts in criminal appeals are more lenient than with civil litigants. The question of jurisdiction, however, can generally be raised at any time because, if the trial court had no jurisdiction, it never should have proceeded to judgment in the first instance.

The initial thing to do, therefore, is to go through the clerk's transcript carefully and see if anything shows up in the papers filed in the case which could be of help. Every once in a while an astute lawyer will get a reversal because some elementary requirement was overlooked either before or during the trial. When you wrote your Statement of the Case, you probably went through the clerk's transcript a bit superficially, so it's worth this second more intensive look.

Then study your Statement of Facts more thoroughly. I always prepare the Statement of Facts with some idea of what my Argument will be. I try to get everything I need out of the record so that I can use it as the basis for the Argument.

Because of the requirement that legal questions must be raised in the trial court in order to be considered on appeal, you will frequently find reported discussions and Points and Authorities in the record which will more or less frame the scope of the issues you will have to cope with. If you tried the case, rereading the record will give you a chance to see everything in perspective for the first time. During the trial, you probably were too involved to make impartial observations.

If you didn't try the case, you probably can be more objective in your evaluation of what points will really be convincing to the reviewing court.

Write the Statement of Facts using a variation on the method you used to prepare for class in law school. First, read the transcript over fast once or twice to get the feel of the case. Witnesses will often testify out of order. Once you know what is in the record, you'll know where the relevant material is and you'll be able to piece it together chronologically and logically. That's when you write it down.

When you finally get to putting down your argument, first outline it so that it reads well. Go for the coronary artery. Put your strongest and most dynamic material right up at the front. Get the judges' attention before you have a chance to lose it. Stick in the boring and minor stuff at the end so that they read it after they're almost convinced. Cover everything in whatever depth is necessary. But remember, you are writing something called a "brief." Go back to the appellate court clerk's office and look over the briefs which won cases. You'll learn a great deal about style, preparation, and argument.

The most important thing in brief writing, however, is intensive research and logical argument. It's your work, preparation, and organization which will win or lose the case. Your insight into new applications of old law will be what benefits your client.

22
ENERGIZING THE BRIEF

Some years ago, I had an interesting briefing problem which at first looked unsolvable. After a lot of thinking and considerable research, however, I was able to create an argument which so intrigued the court that it won the case.

It was in a criminal case. The defendants had been convicted of "conspiracy to injure the public health." On appeal, their counsel raised the issue that the charge was so broad and meaningless as to be constitutionally void due to vagueness.

Intensive research on both sides failed to come up with a case in any jurisdiction, either English or American, which had defined the phrase "injury to the public health." The defense argument was that, under the United States Constitution, the law must be specific enough so that a reasonable person will know whether it is being violated and, if the term has never been defined, no one could know what the elements of the crime were.

With no precedent to follow, I had to take another approach. I remembered from law school that the common law of the United States was all the law of England, both statutes and cases, which existed before the signing of the Declaration of Independence in 1776. Therefore, I decided to trace the statute in question back to see if there was any indication at some time in the past as to how it came to be enacted.

When you are analyzing a statute, always write it out in longhand. It's amazing how certain words suddenly take on new meaning, how punctuation becomes critical, how the very style of the statutory language can cause new ideas to form in your mind, ideas which may give you some clue to the solution of the problem at hand.

That's what happened to me in this case. I noticed that the statute was enacted by the first Legislature of California. The style looked suspiciously as if it had been copied from somewhere else. There was too much detail in it to be something which had just been created out of thin air. I got out the statute books for that first Legislature. My hunch was correct. It was part of a whole enactment devoted to criminal law; it was part of an entire criminal code.

I guessed that some lawyer might have come West in the gold rush of 1849 and brought his law books with him just in case he didn't strike it rich as a miner. I thought perhaps he was elected a member of the first Legislature and proposed a bill which incorporated the criminal code used in his home state. A little research showed me that, possibly, I was on the right track. I discovered that the New York statute on conspiracy was almost word for word the same as California's.

I traced the New York law back to 1829. But I couldn't find any similar language which predated it. I then went into the rare book section of the library and started looking at New York statutes right from the beginning of the colony, when the English took over Manhattan Island from the Dutch. Eventually, I found what I was looking for. Here's how it appeared in the brief:

THE MEANING OF THE TERM
"INJURY TO THE PUBLIC HEALTH"
HAS BEEN WELL KNOWN TO THE
COMMON LAW FOR HUNDREDS OF YEARS

The meaning of the term "injury to the public health" has been well known to the common law for several hundred years. It goes back to the very foundation of the Colony of New York in 1664 when the English took over Manhattan Island from the Dutch.

The Duke of York's Laws for the Government of the Colony of New York were compiled under the direction of the first governor, Richard Nicolls, from existing laws for the government of other English colonies in America. The following statute, sandwiched somewhat alphabetically amidst titles such as "churchwardens," "charges publicke," "children and servants," and material relating to courts, goes right to the heart of "injury to the public health." It became effective in 1665.

"CHIRURGIONS,[1] MIDWIVES, PHYSICIANS.

"That no Person or Persons whatsoever, Employed about the Bed of Men women or Children at any time for preservation of Life or health as Chirurgions, Midwives, Physicians or others; presume to Exercise or put forth any Acte Contrary to the known approved Rules of Art in each mistery or Occupation, or exercise any force, violence or Cruelty upon, or to the Bodies of any whether Young or old; without the advice and Councell of the such as are Skillfull in the same Art (If such may be had,) or at least of some of the wisest and gravest when present and Consent of the patient or patients if they be Mentis Compotes: much less Contrary to such Advice and Consent upon such severe punishments as the nature of the fault may deserve, which Law nevertheless is not intended to discourage any from all Lawfull use of their skill but rather to encourage and direct them in the right use thereof, and to inhibit and restrain the presumptious arogancy of such as through Confidence of their own skill, or any sinister Respect, dare bouldly attempt to Exercise any violence upon or toward the body of young or old one or other, to the prejudice or hazard of the Life or Limb of man, woman, or child." Vol. 1, *The Colonial Laws of New York from the Year 1664 to the Revolution,* pp. 6, 27.

In 1755, New York enacted its first law setting up a ship quarantine area to curtail the spread of infectious and contagious diseases. Van Shaak's Laws, ch. 973; 3 *Colonial Laws of New York,* 1071.

In 1760, the New York Colonial Legislature passed an act to

---

[1] CHIRURGEON is an archaic word for surgeon. *Webster's Third New Int. Dict.* (1961), p. 392.

restrain quacks practicing in the City of New York which act provided for examination and licensing of physicians and surgeons and provided monetary penalties for practicing without the certification. The preamble of that act follows:

"WHEREAS many ignorant and unskilful Persons in Physick and Surgery in order to gain a Subsistence do take upon themselves to administer Physick and practice Surgery in the City of New York to the endangering of the Lives and Limbs of their Patients; and many poor and ignorant Persons inhabiting the said City who have been persuaded to become their Patients have been great Sufferers thereby: For preventing such Abuses for the future, . . ." 4 *Colonial Laws of New York 455,* 1180.

In 1806, the New York State Legislature passed the first medical society act and turned over the examination and licensing of doctors to the profession. The act provided for expulsion of members, if necessary, and that other than grandfather clause practitioners could not thereafter practice unless certified by the society. *Laws of New York,* 29th Session, ch. 138.

It is submitted that the term "any act injurious to the public health" was a well defined phrase at common law and specifically was directed toward (1) quarantine violations, and (2) unnecessary operations and unlicensed practice of medicine which had for their motives avarice and greedy expectation of financial gain or other sinister purposes.

It is also persuasive to note that when the conspiracy statute was initially enacted, everything, after the initial language relating to commission of any offense, was directed to crimes revolving around fraud. And fraud obviously was one of the sinister purposes for which doctors could have been severely punished under the Duke of York Laws and later colonial laws relating to unlicensed practice of medicine.

Finally, the great concern of government that its citizens must be protected from intentional acts obviously injurious to the public health is reflected in the fact that both the Duke of York Laws and the original California statute were each promulgated or enacted at the very time the respective governments were first being established: in New York right after surrender of the Dutch; in California right after the admission of the state.

By the time of oral argument, I found more material which I could use in a little book entitled *His Majesty's Laws for the Plantations of Delaware and Pennsylvania*. Accompanied by an armed library bailiff, I brought that rare old volume to court with me. You should have seen the judges delicately turning the brittle pages! You can read the entire decision in *People* v. *Rehman* (1967) 253 Cal. App. 2d 119, 61 Cal. Rptr. 65.

It's not too often that you can get into legal history so deeply in a brief, but when you have the opportunity, don't let it pass. It brings back memories for the judges of hours of study long years past and they look a bit kindlier on your argument.

23
WHAT KIND OF LAW
TO GO INTO

Most law students have a desire to go into a particular type of law when they get into practice. Unfortunately, the might of realism soon interferes with the dreams of the past. In order to make a living, most lawyers frequently find themselves working in areas they never imagined they'd be involved in when they were in law school.

A law practice evolves from the needs of the clients, not the dreams of the lawyer. And the clients pay the rent. You may have the potential to be the greatest trial lawyer who ever trod the boards of the bar, but if you accidentally happen to fall into a series of uncontested divorces at several hundred dollars a crack, you'll quickly find that that's where your expertise will soon develop. Each happy divorced person you represent will be a walking ad for what a great divorce lawyer you are. Each fee you collect will involve you more deeply in this specialty.

Once in a while, as time goes on, you'll get that big trial which you initially envisioned you'd have every day of your career: but don't look for it to occur too often.

Or it might happen just the other way around. Maybe you wanted to be a big divorce lawyer, yet you find yourself defending cases in court for some insurance company every day.

If you do get what you wished for, consider yourself extremely fortunate—most of your colleagues won't be as lucky.

Essentially, there are three main ways to go: working for somebody else in private practice; working for yourself; working in some institutional type of practice like the government, a corporation, or a poverty law firm, or teaching in a law school.

The "big deal" in American law schools for the past fifty years has been for students to get placed in the prestigious, gigantic law firms, or to get clerkships with appellate and trial court judges. That's practically all the professors and students talk about when job placement is discussed. But those jobs normally go only to the top students in each class. If you can get one, your career will be greatly enhanced.

The really big law firms have so much business that they have to hire people to do the work without worrying whether those persons bring in any new business. A competent, hard-working lawyer with one of these firms can expect to become a partner in a reasonable number of years. Starting salaries are excellent and senior partnership returns are generally in the hundred-thousand-dollars-and-up area.

Young lawyers who get judicial clerkships gain tremendous knowledge and experience as they work up complicated cases for their judges and observe the lawyers of the community in daily practice before the courts. After a few years, they frequently leave for private practice with one of the good, smaller law firms. Their work for the courts gives them great exposure to the successful members of the bar. Here too, as with the big firms, they are associated because there is too much work for existing members of the firm to handle.

About the institutions: If you get on a corporate law staff you'll be on a course leading to an eventual vice-presidency in charge of legal affairs. The timetable is relatively slow; you've got to wait for the people ahead of you to get promoted, retire, or die. The pay is usually good, the hours are better, the fringe benefits are excellent, the responsibility increases with your experience and years of service. About the biggest thing you've got to worry about is the possibility that some new group of outsiders will take over the corporation and you'll be ousted in the resultant merger.

There aren't too many law school teaching positions open. If you manage to obtain one, you'll be hit with the "publish or perish" syndrome. You may find that you have to bounce around from school to school before you get tenure. Salaries are not too bad, and there's great opportunity for consultant work on the side.

Some of the poverty law firms pay fairly well, but many of them think you should be giving a donation for the privilege of representing their clients. The resonsibility comes early and fast. The cases you get may be tiny and numerous or big class actions with great social implications. Opportunity to get into trial and appellate courts is frequent. It's hard to say where you go from there, although private, legal clinic work is a new field which is rapidly opening up, and looks like a natural to fit this kind of experience.

Working for the government is an excellent way to practice. Again, there's a steady progression of promotions, the pay is usually comparable to the private sector, the fringe benefits and vacations are good, and responsibility comes quickly and heavily.

In the federal government, you usually get into administrative law, house counsel advisory work, statutory interpretation, and similar activities. If you're with the United States Attorney General's Office, you go into trial and appellate courts to represent the agencies. If you're with a local United States Attorney's Office, you handle criminal and civil trials. With the federal public defender, you do straight criminal defense work.

At the state levels, there are the attorney general's offices. Most of the criminal work is at the appellate level. The civil work consists of advising agencies, issuing opinions, representing agencies and the state and its officials when they are sued. Some states also have public defenders. There you only write briefs and argue them on appeal.

County district attorney positions give you fantastic experience in trying criminal cases at every level. So do the county public defender offices. County counsel spots take care of all the civil law business for the county. Similarly, some city attorney offices give you this kind of experience. Most cities don't have their own staffs, however. They usually retain outside counsel.

Those individuals who are lucky enough to spend several years in a district attorney's office, spend several in a county counsel's office, and then go into private practice, usually become very successful practitioners in their local communities.

Don't look down on these jobs because some of them may be civil service. You'll find that the clichés about hacks don't apply much any more. Today, this part of the bar is composed of highly competent, dedicated lawyers, many of whom stay for years until they retire. It's the people who work in these government jobs who go to the appellate courts the most.

One common factor in all these institutional jobs which separates them from jobs with small- or medium-sized firms (when you are not a partner) is compensation based on your worth. The government does not have the overhead problems of small firms; it doesn't have to exploit you, intentionally or otherwise, in order to keep you on the payroll.

If you don't connect with any of the above groups, then you have the choice of working for one of the smaller firms or opening your own shop. One of the big problems to be aware of is the tendency for the vast number of medium and smaller law firms to take in a young lawyer with the expectancy, on both sides, that a partnership may result. So many times, however, it doesn't. The young lawyer feels exploited, the firm feels he or she hasn't worked hard enough, and they part with bad feelings on both sides. Sometimes the young lawyer goes to another firm and the same thing happens all over again. Eventually, he or she associates with some other lawyers or practices alone.

Let's take a look at the economics of this for a minute. Assuming good faith on the part of the firm—incidentally, be careful of the possibility that good faith may be absent—find out as much of their past hiring history as possible before you take the job; but, assuming that good faith does exist, let's say they give you x dollars a month to start.

It's almost a certainty that they'll have to lay out another x dollars to pay for your office space, desk, telephone, secretary, social security and unemployment taxes, malpractice insurance, etc. That means that they've already spent 2x dollars on you before you ever get started. And it also means that you have to do as much work as twice what they're paying you for so they can at least break even.

Since the firm is in business to make money, they'll expect you to work still harder at the same pay so that they can get more back from your billable time to the clients. Equating your pay to your work output, you could easily be close to 3x dollars in work for x dollars in pay. This is why it is so common to find young lawyers working in these law firms tremendously long hours at comparatively low pay.

Looking into this situation a little further, we can see that a firm like this cannot afford to take you in as a partner unless you can bring in some business to share with them. Unless you can, you stay on as a wage slave or you quit.

On the other hand, if you work for yourself, every penny you take in is yours. True, you first have to pay your overhead before you can pay yourself, but once that's taken care of, you're ahead for as far as you can go.

One of the biggest thrills in the law business is the day you get your first big fee which is free and clear of any office expenses and which you know is all yours.

A great additional compensation from self-employment, one which you can't put any monetary value on, is the knowledge that you are your own boss. You call the shots. You don't have to march to the beat of anybody else's drum. You give the clients the advice which you know is correct. If you don't like the looks of a client or his ethics, you don't have to do his work. You can tell him to go somewhere else.

But, you are saying, where do I get the clients? I have to work for someone else in order to make a living. In the next chapters, I'll give you some ideas about this which may perhaps give you a different perspective. It's too bad the law schools don't put more emphasis on practicing in your own office.

Even though you can't really tell what type of practice you are headed for, it's wise to keep the type of practice in which you are interested in mind when you choose the electives you take after the first year in law school. In the old days, the curriculum was pretty standardized. Everybody took the same courses for the whole three years. One or two electives were offered for those who felt they had the time. Today, in most schools, everybody takes certain mandatory subjects the first year and then starts running off in all directions.

What kind of electives should you choose? If your grades are really good and it looks like you might be headed for one of those big law firm or judicial clerkship jobs, you'd better stick with the traditional heavies: Future Interests, Advanced Trusts, etc. On the other hand, if you know you're headed for general practice, take those courses which will pay off the quickest: Advanced Criminal Procedure, Family Law Practice, Advanced Civil Procedure, Trial Tactics, Taxation, Wills, Probate Practice, Uniform Commercial Code, Administrative Law, etc. Many of these courses will be taken by almost everyone in the class, but they're especially important if you will be by yourself and are going to handle anything that comes in the front door.

24
HOW TO PICK A PLACE TO PRACTICE

Probably the first and most important consideration is to pick a place to practice where you believe that you'll enjoy the community surroundings and feel secure living among the people who are already there. Over the years, as you progress in your practice, you'll become an important member of this community. And if you want to enjoy life here, you'll have to fit in and accept the local morés and customs.

Quite frequently, however, just like picking the kind of law you go into, deciding on a community is partially based on chance and depends on where you may get a job offer. But keep the community in mind, and if you have serious misgivings, pick someplace else.

Along these lines, you should be aware that there are still a number of states where you can be admitted to the bar without examination if you are already a member in another state. There is a list of places to write to find out about admissions in the *American Jurisprudence 2nd Deskbook,* the last volume of the set.

Remember that, if you're thinking of going in for yourself, a law practice is based on people. The more people who know of you as a lawyer, the more clients you'll have. If you have a big family and lots of friends someplace, think about opening up there. You'll have a built-in referral system that will pay off fairly quickly.

When I first looked for a place to practice, I prepared a résumé of my background and sent it to the presiding judge of each county court in the state, along with a letter asking about the opportunities for practice in his county. Surprisingly, I received personal responses from each of them—some fairly long—giving much valuable information. Some judges gave me a run-down on the various firms, a few suggested places where there might be job opportunities, one even told me of an office for rent where a recently deceased lawyer practiced for twenty years. The most interesting was from a judge who told me he thought a new lawyer could do very well in his county if he were willing to compromise himself and "be a whore for the lumber industry."

I studied Audit Bureau of Circulation reports, Chamber of Commerce publications, and census records at the library to get detailed background on the various places in the state.

As I traveled around looking for a place to light and talked to practicing lawyers and other people in the different communities—storekeepers, teachers, clergy, police officers—I began to get a feeling for where I'd like to be. Finally, everything merged and four cities stood out as ideal locations. I was very satisfied over the years that I made the correct choice.

After I had been in practice for a few years, word got around as to how well I was doing, and I was frequently contacted by newly admitted members of the bar for my views on starting to practice in that locality. This, incidentally, is a good way to get sound information. Most lawyers will take a few minutes to relax and talk shop if you can catch them when they can spare a little time.

One such visit was with a young lawyer who was single and thus free to go practically anywhere. We talked about the two hundred lawyers in my court "trading area," the types of practice most common, usual overhead expenses, fees charged, chances for success, etc. We also discussed the cultural activities available, organizations he might join, nearby recreational facilities, and the like.

During our conversation, I got an idea. I told him that construction on a new dam fifty miles away was going to be started in about six months. The only activity there was engendered by a crossroads country store and bar. A survey crew living in trailers added to the small population. But once the work on the dam started, there would be twenty thousand construction people in the area. I suggested the possibility of his renting a small piece of ground and building a two-room law office up there right outside where the main gate would be. Neither one of us knew whether it would prove to be any good, but he was intrigued with the possibilities and left.

He erected an Abraham-Lincoln-type wooden shack, complete with a porch and a swinging sign bearing his name followed by the word *Lawyer*. For four or five months, as expected, he didn't get much business. Even during that period, however, he did pick up some small contract work and drew a will for one of the local farmers. Then came the inundation. Work on the dam started. Twenty thousand people passed his office twice a day. He was the only lawyer for miles around. And all his clients had ready cash.

Workmen who had been arrested over the weekend for being drunk or fighting in town paid him a fee to appear in court and pay their fines. If they had gone themselves, they would have lost a day's pay. There were divorces, wills, industrial compensation cases, auto accidents, leases—an entire general practice. Suddenly, this newly practicing lawyer was doing better than many of the lawyers who had been around the county seat for a lot longer period of time.

One day, about three years later, as the dam was nearing completion, he stopped in my office to tell me he was moving away to a neighboring state to get married. I asked why he didn't bring his bride down instead. With a chuckle and a twinkle, he replied, "They're building a new dam up there."

I've often thought that a lawyer who opened in one of

the large shopping malls might have similar success. All day long there are several thousand people wandering around who just might have legal problems and would walk into a lawyer's office if one were readily available. If an office were opened there, it would be a good idea to keep evening hours a few nights a week to accommodate the working people also. You'd get to know all the clerks in the stores and they would refer a lot of clients to you.

A location between a busy real estate office and a beauty shop is an excellent location for a lawyer just starting out cold.

Unless you really know a number of people who will send you clients and you decide to go it on your own, you're better off in a street-floor location where passersby will learn of your existence.

While it's nice to be able to practice with a fine library, nice furniture, and a top-notch secretary, it is quite possible to get along with somewhat less. Many of today's successful practitioners started out as young lawyers without even the proverbial nickel. If they had no books, they put up the law school casebooks. Some more audacious ones may even have suggested to their early clients that they practiced the "unwritten law." Others may have let it be known that they never let the authorities prejudice their viewpoints. Most probably were realistic and told their clients that they were just starting out and did their research at the county law library over at the courthouse.

For the bookshelves they did need, they used stained boards propped up on building blocks. For furniture, they got second-hand stuff and refinished it at home. Many did their own typing until they could afford to hire someone to handle the office chores.

I can remember when what must have been the most extreme of shoestring practices existed in the great depression of pre-World War II days. As students, we'd occasionally observe this operation and think it somewhat funny, although now, upon more mature reflection, it appears to have tragic overtones. In New York City's Grand Central Station, there were about fifty lawyers who hung around all day—that was their office. They had cards printed up with their name, post office box number, and the telephone number of a pay phone in the station which always had an "out of order" sign on it. A call would come in. The nearest lawyer would answer it by saying, "Law offices." When the client gave the name of his lawyer, that individual would be called to the telephone. After talking to his client, the lawyer would go to his file, a cardboard box kept in a dime-a-day luggage locker. He typed his letters and pleadings on the ten-cents-an-hour typewriter nearby.

Even in the worst of times, these enterprising souls managed to squeeze out a living for themselves and their families. As long as they had their licenses to practice they could at least earn some income. We hope that such severe challenges to legal ingenuity will never again arise. But the point to remember is that, even if you start small, if you have the desire to practice law and the fortitude to hang in for a while, eventually you'll succeed.

Today, there are many places to get leads on jobs, association possibilities, and places to practice. For example, the little newspapers published at county seats throughout the country which specialize in real estate and court news contain legal notices, court filings, court calendars and dockets, and give general information of interest only to a relatively limited number of people. Often, they will have advertisements for legal positions.

One of the best newspapers for the new lawyer looking for a place to practice or the more experienced lawyer who would like a new place to practice is the *Los Angeles Daily Journal.* Every day it contains two or three full pages of box ads offering legal jobs of all kinds. While most of them are in California, there are some every once in a while for other states as well.

If your grades are high, you probably won't have too

much trouble getting connected somewhere. Generally, the better the job, the bigger the city. As a rule, the big money is in the centers of commerce and industry. In the big cities, too, are the many marginal law firms and individual practices which pick up the crumbs as they fall. In between, of course, are the scores of successful lawyers who the public rarely hears about, but who, through diligent application to their work, give excellent representation to their clients.

In the smaller communities, there are generally several established firms which control most of the good law business in the area. They represent most of the larger businesses and wealthier people. Usually, the senior partners in these firms have long-time roots with interlocking family connections. They're the lawyers who pull the power strings. Frequently, they work behind the scenes and elect the local city and county officials, pick the candidates for the legislature and congress, and control the policies of the major community organizations. They are the lawyers who have the governor's ear when it comes time for judicial appointments, and who stand high on the list themselves for being picked to sit on one of the appellate courts.

But, in all these communities, there is always room for a good young lawyer starting out as a solo practitioner who can successfully handle cases against these establishment firms. A few victories in court, or well-handled negotiations, soon makes them aware of the fresh talent in town, and quite often, when they have something which they cannot handle in their own offices, they will refer a client to someone whom they can trust to reflect favorably on their recommendation.

25
HOW TO GET CLIENTS

If it's your desire to get connected with a firm, corporation, governmental agency, or some other legal enterprise where your paycheck comes in regularly, and you are fortunate enough to be successful in your endeavor, you won't have to worry too much about how to get clients. But if you are discouraged about the job prospects and are even considering the possibility of going it on your own, this chapter is especially for you.

Earlier, I discussed the x-2x-3x-dollar theory of the economics of exploitation of young lawyers. If it looks like you are getting into that kind of a bind, you might want to give serious consideration to opening up your own office instead. Rather than work long hours for low pay at some little outfit, you'd be much better off putting all that energy into something which you were developing for yourself.

And the time to do it is when you're just out of law school. Most of you will be single and, other than some debts you may have accumulated to get through school, you really don't have too many obligations. If things are a little tough in the beginning, the potential is so great that it's worth a try.

Start thinking about a place to practice as early as possible. Even a year before graduation is not too soon. Look over various locations in light of what I outlined in the last chapter. Get the best place your finances will permit. If you have money, be sure to keep some aside to carry you through at the standard you've set for at least a year. If you have none, you've nothing to lose anyway, so don't worry about it.

If you do some careful planning, you might be able to borrow money from a local bank to get started. As long as you can show the banker that you have a future, and are convinced yourself that it really is there, you're a good candidate for a loan.

And since the bank has invested in you, there is a good chance that they will refer business to you. It gives them extra security for the debt you've incurred. Every day, bank customers ask their bankers to recommend a good lawyer for some problem they need handled. The bank itself has a lot of small business which its regular counsel is not set up to take care of properly. For example, there are a number of guardianships under various state and federal progams which require annual accountings to be filed in the local county court. For propriety, the bank prefers to be represented by independent counsel when it asks for a fee out of its ward's guardianship estate. Sometimes, the relative of a deceased depositor will ask the bank to act as administrator of the estate when there is no will. Since the bank will generally give the probate to the lawyer who drew a will, where none exists, the trust officer of the bank has discretion as to what lawyer to get to do the work.

Of course, send out announcements to all your friends and acquaintances. There was a woman I knew who was sure she would go into private practice in her own office when she passed the bar. All through law school, she kept a card index of practically every one she ever met or did business with. And when she sent them announcements she added some little personal note such as, "Met you last year at Harold's house. Drop in and say hi." She never solicited business, but so many people appreciated her friendly manner that she got a number of them as clients and many more referred clients to her. Within a very short time she was running a successful law practice.

Some lawyers go the organization route. They join every group that will take them in. Because of their training and experience, they soon become officers in one or more organizations. The weekly meeting exposure and status makes the members remember they are lawyers, and it's a rare occasion when at least one member doesn't come up to them and ask some legal question. Most of this "banter" is "for free"; however, quite a bit of it turns into something which brings the member into the office as a client.

A great source of business is teaching a "Law for Layman" course at an evening high school or community college. Although a lot of the students are really trying to get advice about their own problems, your answers to their questions whet their appetites and, if they have a serious problem, they will come to you on a professional basis. Also, your students see you standing in front of the class as the great oracle and then tell all their friends and relatives what a great lawyer you are.

At the risk of overindulgence, a lawyer who hits the bars selectively every night on the way home from work picks up a lot of business. One will go to the same bar every night and stay for a few hours, buying drinks and just being a "good guy." Another will go to three or four, staying for one drink at each. The regulars among the customers seem to be the types of people who need lawyers more often than most people, or who have friends and acquaintances who do, and as a consequence they are the source of a lot of business.

The church lawyers achieve the same end in an entirely different way. Because of the high respect they achieve, the congregants look to them as the only lawyers to go to when legal problems arise.

Some lawyers get their clients from people they meet jogging, some from playing golf. It doesn't seem to matter as long as the lawyer is in a place where a number of people over a period of time become used to the idea that "this person is a lawyer, and if I need one, or know someone who does, I will recommend this person to handle the problem."

In some of the larger communities, there are lawyers who handle only misdemeanors. They refer all civil business and felonies to other lawyers who, knowing they will not steal their clients, in turn refer all their misdemeanor clients to them. These lawyers may handle ten or fifteen little cases a day at a reasonable fee, all in cash, and at the end of the year have a gross income in the six-figure range. They have practically no overhead, plead practically all their clients guilty or nolo contendere, or get their cases dismissed instead of going to trial, and frequently are finished with all their court work by eleven o'clock in the morning. Because of their intense specialization, they do an excellent job for their clients and some are highly respected by the courts.

Since the Supreme Court has declared that all persons charged with felonies must be provided with lawyers if they cannot afford them, many counties now have public defenders who handle the cases for these indigents. Frequently, there is a need for additional counsel to represent a codefendant because of possible conflict of interest between the parties. This means that the court must appoint an outside attorney. Many lawyers pick up a considerable amount of money over the years from this source. They are paid from county funds appropriated for the purpose. Talk to the local judges in the places where you look to practice to see how much you could count on if you were to open up an office there.

Along similar lines, check into whether you can be appointed to represent a criminal defendant on appeal. Many states pay appointed counsel to prepare and argue the briefs in those cases.

Another excellent source of legal business is preparation

of income tax returns. Often, this is the first contact many people have with a lawyer. Many of these people will want wills drawn or need other legal work at other times during the year.

Don't overlook the word-of-mouth advertising which you can get from your present clients. Sometimes, they don't even realize they are publicizing you.

I once drew a will for a traveling salesman who stopped in my office as he was passing through town. He asked me to keep the will in my safe, but wondered how his relatives would know about it if anything happened to him while he was on the road. I gave him one of my cards with the following message typed on the back: "In case of accident, serious illness, or death, please contact my lawyer whose name is on the other side of this card." He put his copy of the will in his pocket, put the card in his wallet, and left. Beginning about three weeks later, I started getting a fairly steady stream of new clients from all over the state. It seems that they would meet him in a hotel bar, discuss some legal problem they had, and he would suggest that they see his lawyer, who was so interested in him that he had him keep this card in his wallet just in case anything happened.

Another time, two farmers came in to have a partnership agreement prepared. One had a lease on a piece of ground, the other had the equipment necessary to cultivate it. They wanted "a partnership without clauses." What they meant, of course, was an agreement which an ordinary layman could readily understand. So I prepared something written in simple English which started out like this: "Bill Smith and Charlie Jones want to form a partnership to grow corn. Bill has the lease on eighty acres at the corner of Bradshaw and Marshall Roads. . . ." The complete document was without *whereases, therefores, parties of the first part,* and all the other legal gibberish that most people expect to see in a paper to "make it really legal." It was just what the two men wanted. All the necessary elements of a partnership contract were there, but in language which was completely intelligible to them. Word soon got around, and I became famous in the community as the lawyer who could draw "partnerships without clauses." This one agreement led to almost fifty like it each year from then on.

When people wanted extra copies of wills to send to relatives, I gladly supplied them. Frequently, they came in for wills of their own. This had interesting repercussions one time. An old pensioner I knew came in for a will. He told me that he had starved himself for ten years, but had put a little bit of money away each month and finally invested it in the market, making a killing. He said he had over two hundred thousand dollars on deposit in several savings and loan accounts in town. He wanted to divide all of it between seven nephews and nieces. I prepared the will and, at his request, sent copies to each of the relatives named. Some months later he left the community.

A few years passed. He showed up smoking a good cigar and dressed in a fairly nice suit. He said one of his nieces had given him one that her husband couldn't wear anymore because of too much weight. He then told me that he had lied about the money in the banks; really never had a dime. But he had been visiting each of the seven nephews and nieces on a rotation basis. And life had been really great. Each of them had been trying to outdo the others in hospitality, always hinting that it would be nice to get a larger share of the estate which Uncle Charlie was going to leave. (I didn't send out any more copies of wills after that.)

An excellent source of clients is a political campaign where you are the candidate. It doesn't matter what office you run for (unless perhaps it would be the city attorney of Gomorrah, and even then you'd probably attract all the pro-Gomorrahites), as the name recognition which you'd get would be tremendous. Also, when people become active and support a political candidate, they become very loyal because of their defense of the candidate to voters on the other side; and even if you were to lose, their support would linger on and be demonstrated by the clients they'd refer to your office.

Today, of course, you can advertise directly in newspapers and on radio and television. That's another source to explore, depending on your finances.

Adopt that method of getting clients which best suits your personality. The group of people whom you appeal to will be the basis of your law practice.

SELECTED LAW REVIEW READINGS

NOTE: There are various ways of citing law review articles, depending on how they are being used. Below they are printed in standard bibliographical form. Technical legal writing customarily follows the method set forth in *A Uniform System of Citation*, published by The Harvard Law Review Association, with the author's name in regular roman type, the title of the article in italics, and the name of the law review in large and small capital letters. In the *Index to Legal Periodicals* everything is set in regular type; however, the volume, page, and year appear at the end of the citation, with the volume and page separated by a colon and the year being abbreviated.

ADMINISTRATIVE LAW:

Carrow, "Types of Judicial Relief from Administrative Action," 58 *Colum. L. Rev.* 1 (1958).

Freedman, "Summary Action by Administrative Agencies," 40 *U. Chi. L. Rev.* 1 (1972).

Stewart, "The Reformation of American Administrative Law," 88 *Harv. L. Rev.* 1669 (1975).

Zamir, "Administrative Control of Administrative Action," 57 *Calif. L. Rev.* 866 (1969).

AGENCY:

Seavey, "Subagents and Subservants," 68 *Harv. L. Rev.* 658 (1954).

COMMERCIAL LAW:

Benson and Squillante, "Role of the Holder in Due Course Doctrine in Consumer Credit Transactions," 26 *Hastings L. J.* 427 (1974).

Danzig, "A Comment on the Jurisprudence of the Uniform Commercial Code," 27 *Stan. L. Rev.* 621 (1975).

Friedman, "Formative Elements in the Law of Sales: The Eighteenth Century," 44 *Minn. L. Rev.* 363 (1960).

Llewellyn, "Across Sales on Horseback," 52 *Harv. L. Rev.* 725 (1939).

Llewellyn, "The First Struggle to Unhorse Sales," 52 *Harv. L. Rev.* 873 (1939).

Palmer, "Negotiable Instruments under the Uniform Commercial Code," 48 *Mich. L. Rev.* 255 (1950).

Schmitt and Johnson, "A Poker Player's Guide to Uniform Commercial Code Secured Transactions," 10 *Sw. Nev. L. Rev.* 2089 (1978).

"Uniform Commercial Code," 16 *Law and Contemp. Prob.* 1-346 (1951).

CONFLICT OF LAWS:

Barrett, "The Doctrine of Forum Non Conveniens," 35 *Calif. L. Rev.* 380 (1947).

Cook, " 'Immovables' and the 'Law' of the 'Situs,' " 52 *Harv. L. Rev.* 1246 (1939).

Ehrenzweig, "Contracts in Conflict of Laws," 59 *Colum. L. Rev.* 973, 1171 (1959).

Ehrenzweig, "The Lex Fori—Basic Rule in the Conflict of Laws," 58 *Mich. L. Rev.* 637 (1960).

Ehrenzweig, "The Statute of Frauds in the Conflict of Laws," 59 *Colum. L. Rev.* 874 (1959).

Ehrenzweig, "Torts, Contracts, Property, Status, Characterization and the Conflict of Laws," 59 *Colum. L. Rev.* 440 (1959).

Gorfinkel, "Conflict of Laws—A Survey of Past and Contemporary Theory," 16 *Hastings L. J.* 21 (1964).

Griswold, "Renvoi Revisited," 51 *Harv. L. Rev.* 1165 (1938).

Lorenzen, "Developments in Conflict of Laws, 1902–1942," 40 *Mich. L. Rev.* 781 (1942).

Reese, "Does Domicile Bear a Single Meaning?" 55 *Colum. L. Rev.* 589 (1955).

Reese and Flesch, "Agency and Vicarious Liability in Conflict of Laws," 60 *Colum. L. Rev.* 764 (1960).

Scoles, "Apportionment of Federal Estate Taxes and Conflict of Laws," 55 *Colum. L. Rev.* 261 (1955).

Shulman and Prevezer, "Torts in English and American Conflict of Laws: The Role of the Forum," 56 *Mich. L. Rev.* 1067 (1958).

Stern, "Foreign Law in the Courts," 45 *Calif. L. Rev.* 23 (1957).

Misc., "Comments on *Babcock* v. *Jackson,* A Recent Development in Conflict of Laws," 63 *Colum. L. Rev.* 1212 (1963).

CONSTITUTIONAL LAW:

Avins, "The Fifteenth Amendment and Literacy Tests: The Original Intent," 18 *Stan. L. Rev.* 808 (1966).

Berney, "Libel and the First Amendment—A New Constitutional Privilege," 51 *Va. L. Rev.* 1 (1965).

Fairman, "Does the Fourteenth Amendment Incorporate the Bill of Rights?" 2 *Stan. L. Rev.* 5 (1949).

Frank and Munro, "The Original Understanding of 'Equal Protection of the Laws,' " 50 *Colum. L. Rev.* 131 (1950).

Granucci, " 'No Cruel and Unusual Punishments Inflicted': The Original Meaning," 57 *Calif. L. Rev.* 839 (1969).

Henderson, "The Background of the Seventh Amendment," 80 *Harv. L. Rev.* 289 (1966).

Howe, "The Meaning of 'Due Process of Law' Prior to the Adoption of the Fourteenth Amendment," 18 *Calif. L. Rev.* 583 (1930).

Johnston, "Sex Discrimination and the Supreme Court," 49 *N.Y.U. L. Rev.* 617 (1974).

Lewis, "The Meaning of State Action," 60 *Colum. L. Rev.* 1083 (1960).

Mendelson, "Mr. Justice Frankfurter on the Construction of Statutes," 43 *Calif. L. Rev.* 652 (1955).

Mosk, "The Eighth Amendment Rediscovered," 1 *Loy. L. Rev.* 4 (1968).

Oaks, "Legal History in the High Court—Habeas Corpus," 64 *Mich. L. Rev.* 451 (1966).

Ratner, "The Function of the Due Process Clause," 116 *U. Pa. L. Rev.* 1048 (1968).

Rogge, "Unenumerated Rights (The Ninth Amendment)," 47 *Calif. L. Rev.* 787 (1959).

Ruud, "One-subject Rule," 42 *Minn. L. Rev.* 389 (1958).

ten Broeck, "Admissibility and Use by the United States Supreme Court of Extrinsic Aids in Constitutional Construction," 26 *Calif. L. Rev.* 287, 437, 664 (1938); 157, 399 (1939).

Van Alstyne and Karst, "State Action," 14 *Stan. L. Rev.* 3 (1961).

Wilkinson, "The Supreme Court, the Equal Protection Clause, and the Three Faces of Constitutionality," 61 *Va. L. Rev.* 945 (1975).

Wolfram, "Constitutional History of the Seventh Amendment," 57 *Minn. L. Rev.* 639 (1973).

"The Right to Counsel: A Symposium," 45 *Minn. L. Rev.* 693-896 (1961).

CONTRACTS:

Blake, "Employee Agreements Not to Compete," 73 *Harv. L. Rev.* 625 (1960).

Boyer, "Promissory Estoppel," 50 *Mich. L. Rev.* 639, 873 (1952).

Childres, "Conditions in the Law of Contracts," 45 *N.Y.U. L. Rev.* 33 (1970).

Childres and Spitz, "Status in the Law of Contract," 47 *N.Y.U. L. Rev.* 1 (1972).

Corbin, "Recent Developments in the Law of Contracts," 50 *Harv. L. Rev.* 449 (1937).

Dawson, "Economic Duress—An Essay in Perspective," 45 *Mich. L. Rev.* 251 (1947).

Farnsworth, "Disputes Over Omission in Contracts," 68 *Colum. L. Rev.* 860 (1968).

Farnsworth, "Implied Warranties of Quality in Non-sales Cases," 57 *Colum. L. Rev.* 653 (1957).

Farnsworth, " 'Meaning' in the Law of Contracts," 76 *Yale L. J.* 939 (1967).

Farnsworth, "The Past of Promise: An Historical Introduction to Contract," 69 *Colum. L. Rev.* 576 (1969).

Ferson, "Contracts in Favor of Third Parties," 6 *Hastings L. J.* 354 (1955).

Henderson, "Promissory Estoppel and Traditional Contract Doctrine," 78 *Yale L. J.* 343 (1969).

Horwitz, "The Historical Foundations of Modern Contract Law," 87 *Harv. L. Rev.* 917 (1974).

Kepner, "Part Performance in Relation to Parol Contracts for the Sale of Lands," 35 *Minn. L. Rev.* 1 (1950).

McCall, "Repossession and Adhesion Contract Issues," 26 *Hastings L. J.* 383 (1974).

McGovern, "The Enforcement of Oral Covenants Prior to Assumpsit," 65 *Nw.U. L. Rev.* 576 (1970).

Palmer, "Reformation and the Parol Evidence Rule," 65 *Mich. L. Rev.* 833 (1967).

Paterson, "Freak-Tent of Contracts," 1 *Hastings L. J.* 141 (1950).

Patterson, "An Apology for Consideration," 58 *Colum. L. Rev.* 929 (1958).

Patterson, "The Interpretation and Construction of Contracts," 64 *Colum. L. Rev.* 833 (1964).

Rosett, "Contract Performance: Promises, Conditions and the Obligation to Communicate," 22 *U.C.L.A. L. Rev.* 1083 (1975).

Trimble, "The Law Merchant and the Letter of Credit," 61 *Harv. L. Rev.* 981 (1948).

CORPORATIONS:

Berger, " 'Disregarding the Corporate Entity' for Stockholders' Benefit," 55 *Colum. L. Rev.* 808 (1955).

Conrad, "An Overview of the Laws of Corporations," 71 *Mich. L. Rev.* 621 (1973).

Mazumdar, "The Modern Corporation and the Rule of Law," 114 *U.Pa. L. Rev.* 187 (1965).

CRIMES:

Blume, "The Place of Trial of Criminal Cases," 43 *Mich. L. Rev* 59 (1944).

Calkins, "Grand Jury Secrecy," 63 *Mich. L. Rev.* 455 (1965).

Fletcher, "The Metamorphosis of Larceny," 89 *Harv. L. Rev.* 469 (1976).

Herman, "Warrants for Arrest or Search: Impeaching the Allegations of a Facially Sufficient Affidavit," 36 *Ohio St. L. J.* 721 (1975).

Oberer, "The Deadly Weapon Doctrine: Common Law Origin," 75 *Harv. L. Rev.* 1532 (1962).

Perkins, "The Act of One Conspirator," 26 *Hastings L. J.* 337 (1974).

Perkins, "An Analysis of Assault and Attempts to Assault," 47 *Minn. L. Rev.* 71 (1962).

Perkins, "A Rationale of Mens Rea," 52 *Harv. L. Rev.* 905 (1939).

Perkins, "The Territorial Principle in Criminal Law," 22 *Hastings L. J.* 1155 (1971).

Silten and Tullis, "Mental Competency in Criminal Proceedings," 28 *Hastings L. J.* 1053 (1977).

Smith, "Two Problems in Criminal Attempts," 70 *Harv. L. Rev.* 422 (1957).

EQUITY:

Chafee, "Coming into Equity with Clean Hands," 47 *Mich. L. Rev.* 877, 1065 (1949).

Chesnin and Hazard, "Chancery Procedure and the Seventh Amendment: Jury Trial of Issues in Equity Cases before 1791," 83 *Yale L. J.* 999 (1974).

Newman, "The Hidden Equity," 19 *Hastings L. J.* 147 (1967).

Newman, "What Light is Cast by History on the Nature of Equity in Modern Law?" 17 *Hastings L. J.* 677 (1966).

Simpson, "Fifty Years of American Equity," 50 *Harv. L. Rev.* 171 (1936).

ETHICS:

Curtis, "Ethics in the Law," 4 *Stan. L. Rev.* 477 (1952).

Curtis, "The Ethics of Advocacy," 4 *Stan. L. Rev.* 3 (1952).

EVIDENCE:

Goodhart, "A Changing Approach to the Law of Evidence," 51 *Va. L. Rev.* 759 (1965).

FUTURE INTERESTS:

Dukeminier, "Contingent Remainders and Executory Interests," 43 *Minn. L. Rev.* 13 (1958).

Leach, "Perpetuities in Perspective: Ending the Rule's Reign of Terror," 65 *Harv. L. Rev.* 721 (1951).

Leach, "Perpetuities: The Nutshell Revisited," 78 *Harv. L. Rev.* 973 (1965).

Leach and Logan, "Perpetuities: A Standard Savings Clause to Avoid Violations of the Rule," 74 *Harv. L. Rev.* 1141 (1961).

Powell, "The Rule Against Perpetuities and Spendthrift Trusts in New York," 71 *Colum. L. Rev.* 688 (1971).

LANDLORD AND TENANT:

Love, "Landlord's Liability for Defective Premises," 1975 *Wis. L. Rev.* (19–).

LEGAL HISTORY:

Braybrooke, "Custom as a Source of English Law," 50 *Mich. L. Rev.* 71 (1951).

Green, "The Jury and the English Law of Homicide," 74 *Mich. L. Rev.* 413 (1976).

Noonan, "The Steady Man: Process and Policy in the Courts of the Roman Curia," 58 *Calif. L. Rev.* 628 (1970).

Pound, "The Role of the Will in Law," 68 *Harv. L. Rev.* 1 (1954).

Smith, "Administrative Control of the Courts of the American Plantations," 61 *Colum. L. Rev.* 121 (1961).

MOOT COURT:

Honigman, "The Art of Appellate Advocacy," 64 *Mich. L. Rev.* 1055 (1966).

Marer, "Effective Criminal Appellate Advocacy," 27 *Hastings L. J.* 333 (1975).

Smith, "A Primer of Opinion Writing for Law Clerks," 26 *Vand. L. Rev.* 1203 (1973).

PLEADING AND PRACTICE:

Semmel, "Collateral Estoppel, Mutuality and Joinder of Parties," 68 *Colum. L. Rev.* 1457 (1968).

PROPERTY:

Browder, "Rule Against Perpetuities," 62 *Mich. L. Rev.* 1 (1963).

Hogan, "The Innkeepers Lien at Common Law," 8 *Hastings L. J.* 33 (1956).

Lund, "Early American Wildlife Law," 51 *N.Y.U. L. Rev.* 703 (1976).

McGovern, "The Historical Conception of a Lease for Years," 23 *U.C.L.A. L. Rev.* 501 (1976).

Newman and Losey, "Covenants Running with the Land and Equitable Servitude," 21 *Hastings L. J.* 1319 (1970).

Paulus, *"Finder* v. *Locus,* in Quo—An Outline," 6 *Hastings L. J.* 180 (1955).

Rabin, "The Law Favors the Vesting of Estates. Why?" 65 *Colum. L. Rev.* 467 (1965).

QUASI-CONTRACTS:

Perillo, "Restitution in a Contractual Context," 73 *Colum. L. Rev.* 1208 (1973).

RESTITUTION:

Thurston, "Recent Developments in Restitution 1940–1947," 45 *Mich. L. Rev.* 935 (1947).

Thurston, "Recent Developments in Restitution: Recission and Reformation for Mistake, Including Misrepresentation," 46 *Mich. L. Rev.* 1037 (1948).

TAXATION:

Browder, "Trusts and the Doctrine of Estates," 72 *Mich. L. Rev.* 1507 (1974).

TORTS:

Calabresi, "Concerning Cause and the Law of Torts," 43 *U.Chi. L. Rev.* 69 (1975).

Calabresi and Hirschoff, "Toward a Test for Strict Liability in Torts," 81 *Yale L. J.* 1055 (1972).

Gordon, "The Unborn Plaintiff," 63 *Mich. L. Rev.* 579 (1965).

Green, "The Causal Relation Issue in Negligence Law," 60 *Mich. L. Rev.* 543 (1962).

James and Thornton, "Impact of Insurance on the Law of Torts," 15 *Law and Contemp. Prob.* 431 (1950).

Keeton, "Conditional Fault in the Law of Torts," 72 *Harv. L. Rev.* 401 (1959).

Keeton, "Trespass, Nuisance and Strict Liability," 59 *Colum. L. Rev.* 457 (1959).

Prosser, "Comparative Negligence," 51 *Mich. L. Rev.* 465 (1953).

Prosser, "False Imprisonment: Consciousness of Confinement," 55 *Colum. L. Rev.* 847 (1955).

Prosser, "Injurious Falsehood: The Basis of Liability," 59 *Colum. L. Rev.* 425 (1959).

Prosser, "Insult and Outrage," 44 *Calif. L. Rev.* 40 (1956).

Prosser, "Palsgraf Revisited," 52 *Mich. L. Rev.* 1 (1953).

Prosser, "Privacy," 48 *Calif. L. Rev.* 383 (1960).

Seavey, "Nuisance: Contributory Negligence and Other Mysteries," 65 *Harv. L. Rev.* 984 (1951).

Stone, "Touchstones of Tort Liability," 2 *Stan. L. Rev.* 259 (1950).

TRUSTS:

Scott, "The Fiduciary Principle," 37 *Calif. L. Rev.* 539 (1949).

Scott, "Restitution from an Innocent Transferee Who Is Not a Purchaser for Value," 62 *Harv. L. Rev.* 1022 (1948).

WILLS:

Halbach, "Stare Decisis and Rules of Construction in Wills and Trusts," 52 *Calif. L. Rev.* 921 (1964).

McGovern, "Homicide and Succession to Property," 68 *Mich. L. Rev.* 65 (1969).

Pound, "The Role of the Will in Law," 68 *Harv. L. Rev.* 1 (1954).

Sparks, "Enforcement of Contracts to Devise or Bequeath After the Death of the Promisor," 39 *Minn. L. Rev.* 1 (1954).

MISCELLANEOUS:

Cahn, "Authority and Responsibility," 51 *Colum. L. Rev.* 839 (1951).

Cappelletti and Gordley, "Legal Aid: Modern Theories and Variations," 24 *Stan. L. Rev.* 347 (1972).

Christie, "Vagueness and Legal Language," 48 *Minn. L. Rev.* 885 (1964).

Cohen, "Thoman Jefferson Recommends A Course of Law Study," 119 *U.Pa. L. Rev.* 823 (1971).

Finkelstein and Fairley, "A Comment on Trial by Mathematics," 84 *Harv. L. Rev.* 1801 (1971).

Hancock, " 'In the Parish of St. Mary Le Bow, in the Ward of Cheap,' " 16 *Stan. L. Rev.* 516 (1964).

Hills, "The Law of Accounting," 54 *Colum. L. Rev.* 1, 1049 (1954).

Kenyon, "Legal Lore of the Wild West. A Bibliographical Essay," 56 *Calif. L. Rev.* 681 (1968).

Nagel and Weitzman, "Women as Litigants," 23 *Hastings L. J.* 171 (1971).

Newman, "Similarity of Doctrines in Legal Systems," 18 *Hastings L. J.* 481 (1967).

Shapiro, "Law and Science in Seventeenth-Century England," 21 *Stan. L. Rev.* 722 (1969).

Silving, "The Unknown and Unknowable in Law," 35 *Calif. L. Rev.* 352 (1947).

Stein, "The Attraction of the Civil Law in Post-Revolutionary America," 52 *Va. L. Rev.* 403 (1966).

Stevens, "Law Schools and Law Students," 59 *Va. L. Rev.* 551 (1973).

Stone, "Legal Education on the Couch," 85 *Harv. L. Rev.* 392 (1971).

Touster, "Holmes: The Years of the Common Law," 64 *Colum. L. Rev.* 230 (1964).

Tribe, "Further Critique of Mathematical Proof," 84 *Harv. L. Rev.* 1810 (1971).

Tribe, "Trial by Mathematics: Precision and Ritual in the Legal Process," 84 *Harv. L. Rev.* 1329 (1971).

Trubek, "Toward a Social Theory of Law: An Essay on the Study of Law and Development," 82 *Yale L. J.* 1 (1972).

White, "The Rise and Fall of Justice Holmes," 39 *U.Chi. L. Rev.* 51 (1971).

Williams, "The Concept of Legal Liberty," 56 *Colum. L. Rev.* 1129 (1956).

"The Common Law Origins of the Infield Fly Rule," 123 *U.Pa. L. Rev.* 1474 (1975).

"Uniformity in Financial Accounting," 30 *Law and Contemp. Prob.* 621–931 (1965).

GLOSSARY OF LEGAL TERMS

Here is a list of some of the words and phrases you'll run into at law school. They're defined in nonlegal language to make it easier for you to do your preliminary orientation reading. When you actually get into your casebooks, be sure to look up the precise definitions in your law dictionary.

abandon: give up all claims or rights to something
abate: put an end to some situation
abet: urge someone to commit a criminal act
ab initio: going back to the beginning
absentee: individual who is not present
abstract: short version of a case or of a public record
abut: adjacent to
accept: knowingly receive or agree
acceptance: response to an offer in anticipation of entering into a contract
accession: increase in real or personal property
accessory: party to a criminal act
accessory after the fact: person aiding a criminal after the commission of the crime
accessory before the fact: being absent, but participating in the planning of a crime
accident: an injury for which there is no legal remedy
accomplice: party to a criminal act
accord and satisfaction: settlement of a claim for less than the full amount
account stated: an agreement between debtor and creditor as to the balance due
accretion: gradual increase in the size of land adjacent to water because of silt, rock, or sand
accrue: reach a certain point in time or growth
acknowledgment: declaration before a notary public that the maker has signed a document

acquittal: finding of not guilty in a criminal case

action: a suit in the law or equity courts

actionable negligence: conduct which gives rise to an action in tort for damages

action at law: a case coming before the law courts

action in equity: a case coming before the equity courts

action on the case: action at common law for damages where no willful force was used

act of God: event which occurs without human intervention

act of law: governmental intervention which interferes with intentions of parties dealing with each other

adeem: to diminish a legacy because of gifts prior to death

administrative agency: a governmental agency which makes and enforces rules and regulations in a specialized field

administrative law: branch of law dealing with regulations by, and hearings before, administrative agencies

advance sheets: interim paperback supplements to volumes of reported cases, containing new cases, which latter are incorporated in a new volume when the quantity is sufficient

adverse possession: holding real property without benefit of a deed

affirmance: appellate court ruling that the lower court correctly tried the case

affirmative duty: special duty required by law in conduct toward others

aiding and abetting: being present and helping commit a crime without actually taking part in the criminal act itself

allegation: statement of fact in a pleading

annotation: citations following a statute showing the cases where the statute has been mentioned

answer: written document responding to the allegations of a complaint

asportation: taking of goods illegally

assault: attempt to commit a battery which falls short of actually touching the intended victim

assumpsit: action on a contract at common law

at issue: case is ready for trial

attempt: an act intended to culminate in a crime, which act is never finalized by commission of the crime

bail: a sum of money or other security deposited in court to guarantee a person's appearance for trial

battery: trespass to the person where there is an actual touching

beneficiary: individual benefiting from a trust or contract made by other parties

bequest: gift of personal property made in a will

bilateral contract: contract in which both parties are bound to do something

blackacre: used to describe a hypothetical parcel of land in real property class discussions

bona fide: good faith

brief: a written legal argument submitted to an appellate court

burden of proof: the duty on the part of a litigant to convince the trier of fact that his or her side of the case should prevail

burglary: at common law, breaking into a dwelling at night

case: a lawsuit generally; also, a particular action at common law to recover money damages

casebook: law school book containing reported appellate cases on a particular subject arranged to present an orderly development of that area of law

case in point: a case pertaining to the rule of law under consideration

case law: the law found in the decisions of the appellate courts

cause: a lawsuit

caveat emptor: let the buyer beware

chancery: the courts of equity

citation: volume, page, and reporter where a case may be found

code: group of statutes, usually consolidated by subject

common law: law developed by judges through written opinions

common law pleading: the entire system of presenting the facts and issues of a case to a court through documents filed before the trial started

comparative negligence: a doctrine in the law of torts where the jury assesses the damages based upon its finding as to what percentage of fault it allocates to each party

complainant: the person instituting a suit in an action at law

complaint: initial document filed in a lawsuit

compounding a felony: victim agreeing not to prosecute in exchange for being repaid or bribed not to testify

confession and avoidance: a common law pleading admitting the facts alleged but adding something new to alter the interpretation of those facts

conflict of laws: a branch of the law dealing with the law to be applied by the court when the events of the case occurred in two states

consideration: the ultimate basis of a contract; some act or promise given in exchange for another act or promise

conspiracy: agreement between two or more persons to commit some illegal act

contract: a legally enforceable agreement

contributory negligence: an act by the plaintiff which contributed to the injury

conveyance: a deed

close: the land and buildings around a dwelling house

county court: local trial court

crime: violation of some law which is punishable by some governmental entity

cross offers: offers relating to the same subject matter sent by opposing parties to each other simultaneously

damages: amount of money awarded to the victorious plaintiff in a lawsuit

decedent: a dead person

decedent's estate: a dead person's assets subject to the jurisdiction of a probate court

decision: the court determination as to which side won the lawsuit

defendant: the person sued in an action at law

demurrer: a pleading which in effect admits the facts alleged in the complaint but argues that even if they are true, the complaint fails to state a cause of action

digest: set of index books containing the headnotes of a particular series of reports arranged by legal topic

dilatory plea: a plea at common law which could stop the case from proceeding until the point raised was cleared up

district court: the lowest court in the federal trial system

domicile: a person's permanent home

easement: right to use another's land in a certain manner

elements of a cause of action: those things which must be alleged and proved in order to show that the plaintiff has a valid cause of action

entrapment: tricking someone into committing a crime

equity: that branch of law dealing with the court's right to give remedies other than money damages

estate: a right in real property; an individual's assets

exception: in the older cases, the trial lawyer had to object, and then take exception to a judge's ruling, if he wished to preserve the right to contest the ruling on appeal

execution of judgment: enforcement of the ruling of a court

exhaustion of administrative remedies: legal doctrine that prevents a person from suing in court on a matter within the province of an administrative agency until all remedies permitted by the agency are first taken

false imprisonment: confining someone's ability to move about freely without any legal right to keep the person restricted

federal court: a court in the federal judicial system

fee: title to land

fee simple: full title to land

felony: a serious crime punishable by imprisonment or death

feudal system: the ancient English method of land ownership and allegiance to the king through a pyramidal system running through serfs through their knights, through various higher nobles, up to the ruler

first degree murder: killing with intent, premeditation and deliberation

fixtures: personal property items attached to realty

foreseeable: a reasonable man could anticipate the consequences

future interests: a branch of the law of real property dealing with the rights of persons coming after the grantor and grantee

general damages: estimated damages set by the jury, over and above actual out-of-pocket expenses, arising as a result of the defendant's conduct

general intent: criminal law concept which allows certain crimes to be proven even though no specific intent is shown

gift: something of value transferred to another without consideration

grand jury: group of people chosen in a county by the court who hand down indictments for crimes

granted: court ruling upholding a motion

grantee: person named to receive property in a deed

grantor: maker of a deed

guaranty: agreement to pay another's debt if the debtor defaults

guardian: person appointed by a court to take care of the person or estate of someone not legally qualified to do so

headnotes: summaries of points of law contained in an opinion generally coded to the text for easy reference

heir: person who succeeds to a decedent's estate under the inheritance laws

holding: the rule of a case

hypothetical: made-up set of facts to test a legal principle

in camera: privately heard by a judge in chambers

indebitatus assumpsit: action on a contract at common law

indictment: finding by a grand jury that they have heard enough evidence to believe a person should be brought to trial for a crime which has been committed

infancy: under age

infra: reference in a citation to indicate that the case will be cited again in the same opinion

in personam: jurisdiction over a person

in rem: jurisdiction over property or other subject matter in an action

interim: temporary

interlocutory: interim order of a court temporarily deciding some phase of a case

intermediate appellate court: a court above a trial court but below the supreme court

intervening cause: tort concept excusing original conduct when a new independent cause of the injury exists

intestate: dying without leaving a valid will

involuntary manslaughter: killing through extreme recklessness

issue: children; the legal point in a case; handing down an order in a case

jurisdiction: the right of a court to hear a case or to issue an order

jurisprudence: philosophy of the law

jury: twelve people who decide innocence or guilt in a criminal case, or the winner and amount of damages in a civil case

last clear chance: tort doctrine which excuses the injury if the victim had time to avoid it

law review: legal journal put out periodically by students under faculty direction which comments on developments in the law

leave to amend: court's permission to change a pleading

liability without fault: tort concept imposing liability because of the ultra-hazardous nature of the activity

liable: legally obligated to pay damages for the consequences of some act

litigant: party to a lawsuit

litigation indices: court clerk's files of cases indexed by names of plaintiffs and defendants

local court: state trial court

lower court: trial court

malum in se: conduct which is criminal because inherently wrong

malum prohibitum: conduct which is criminal because it violates some statute or ordinance

meeting of the minds: both sides are talking about the same thing

minor: person below the age of legally being able to consent to something or to enter into some legally recognized activity

misdemeanor: crime punishable by fine or local jail incarceration for term under one year

motion: request for some interim ruling from a court during pendency of a lawsuit

negligence: conduct which disregards the proper standard of care to be expected under the circumstances

nominal damages: small amount of damages awarded as a token

offer: first step looking toward an agreement which will materialize into a contract

opinion: written decision of an appellate court

option: contract to keep an offer open for a certain period of time

order: action taken by a judge in ruling on a motion; direction by a court that something be done by someone connected with a lawsuit

order to show cause: court order directing someone to appear in court on a certain date and justify why they should be allowed to continue a certain course of conduct

ordinance: law enacted by a local legislative body such as a board of supervisors or city council

overruled: court ruling against a demurrer or motion

person: an individual

personal property: moveable goods or chattels, as opposed to real property or land

petition: initial document filed in an action in equity

pleading: technical legal document filed in an action which tells what a certain part of the case is about

plea in bar: pleading which stops the progress of a case because of a technicality

pocket parts: paperback supplements to hard-covered law books which fit inside the rear cover and show changes and additions since the volume was printed

points and authorities: written legal arguments submitted to a trial court

privity of contract: in direct contractual relationship with another

probate court: special equity court which administers wills and decedents' estates

proceedings: the activities in the equity courts

proximate cause: event which is the direct cause of an injury

public policy: what the court believes the community attitude is toward certain behavior

punitive damages: amount of money over and above actual damages awarded as an extra penalty to victorious plaintiff in a lawsuit

quasi contracts: law relating to suits for unjust enrichment

quitclaim deed: deed transferring whatever interest grantor has in the property

real property: land, as opposed to personal property

reasonable man: the hypothetical standard of care in negligence cases which varies depending on circumstances

rebutter: defendant's third pleading at common law

record: the contents of a case file; the transcript of testimony, and evidence in a case

reeve: a local officer in the English judicial system

rejoinder: common law pleading amending defendant's answer to an amended complaint or replication

replication: common law pleading amending a complaint after a successful demurrer

reports: series of volumes containing cases decided by appellate courts within a particular jurisdiction

res ipsa loquitur: tort doctrine which forces defendant to explain how the injury occurred

retroactivity: constitutional law doctrine that applies new court decision to older cases

robbery: theft from the person by force and fear

rule of law: a legal principle, accepted as such by the knowledgeable people in the specialized field in which it appears

ruling: the decision of a court on a motion; or a point of law made in a decision

second degree murder: killing with intent, but without premeditation or deliberation

shire: English political subdivision corresponding to an American county

solicitation: the crime of asking someone to commit a crime

special damages: the out-of-pocket expenses necessitated by a tort

specific intent: criminal law concept which must be proven by the prosecution in order to convict of certain crimes

state court: any court of a state

statute: law enacted by the highest legislative body in a jurisdiction, such as Parliament, Congress, or a state legislature

statute of frauds: English law requiring that certain contracts be in writing to be enforceable in an action at law

statutory law: statutes passed by legislative bodies

stay of execution: court order preventing enforcement of a judgment for some temporary period

stipulation: formal agreement by the parties relating to something concerning a lawsuit

subpoena: court order directing someone to appear as a witness

subpoena duces tecum: court order directing someone to bring written documents to court

substantive law: law of particular subjects, i.e. contracts, torts, real property

supra: reference in a citation to indicate that the case was previously cited in the same opinion

surrebutter: plaintiff's fourth pleading at common law

sustained: court ruling upholding a demurrer

temporary restraining order: an order issued by a trial court directing someone to refrain from doing something until the court has had a chance to decide a lawsuit

testate: dead, leaving a valid will

tort: injury to a person or to property which gives rise to a cause of action for money damages

transcript: stenographic record of the testimony in a case

traverse: denial of facts alleged in the original pleading

trespass: entering on someone's land without permission; doing something illegal to another person's property; unlawfully injuring another; name of a common law action

trespass on the case: sometimes called "action on the case," or "case"; form of common law pleading in tort where no willful force was involved

trespass de bonis asportatis: trespass to personal property

trespass quare clausum fregit: trespass to land

trial by battel: an ancient form of trial in a civil case where the parties, through representatives, engaged in a technically structured joust to determine the victor in the litigation

trial by oath: an ancient form of trial where witnesses took an oath that they believed the defendant

trial by ordeal: an ancient form of trial by torture in a criminal case where the defendant was acquitted if he survived

trial court: court which hears witnesses and takes evidence in a case

ubi supra: reference to cases previously cited in an opinion

uniform laws: similar codes of laws adopted by several states

unilateral contract: contract in which only the offeror is bound, provided the offeree does the required act in response to the offer

upper court: appellate court

voluntary manslaughter: killing without intent under extreme provocation

wager of battel: same as trial by battel; physical combat to decide outcome of a lawsuit

waiver: giving up of some right

warrant: court order directing someone's arrest

within the four corners: contained either expressly or by implication within the text of a document

writ: the initial document filed to commence an action at law or in equity; an order of a court directing someone to do something